Minnesota Vikings

Facts & Trivia

by

John Holler

Ravenstone Publishing Group, Inc.
Berlin, Wisconsin
est. 1998

Ravenstone Publishing Group, Inc.
162 W. Huron
Berlin, WI 54923

ISBN: 0-9667300-0-3

Library of Congress Card Catalog Number: 98-068222

First Printing: November 1998

Printed in USA

Cover Photo by Ben Johnson/Viking Update

All text photos courtesy of Viking Update

TABLE OF CONTENTS

To Mom and Dad,

who always believed in me;

To Bob and Tony,

Who opened doors I could have never opened myself;

To Dawn and Megan,

Who taught me that love is more important than money or fame;

To all of you, for different reasons, this book is dedicated.

Minnesota
Vikings
Facts & Trivia

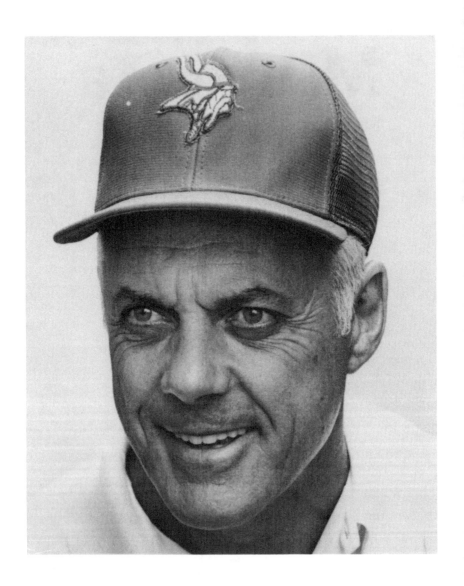

Bud Grant

Introduction

O ver the course of a lifetime, everybody meets their one true love. Whether it be a soul-mate that one spends the golden years growing old with or a flame that flickers out too soon but burns a permanent memory in the heart, the love remains and grows stronger even as memories fade.

For nearly four decades, football fans from Minnesota, Iowa, the Dakotas and points from Washington to Florida, California to Maine and countless cities and towns in between have maintained a love affair with the Minnesota Vikings. Unlike allegiances to many of professional sports franchises, relocation rarely wanes the interest of a fan smitten by the allure of the Minnesota Vikings. As the rationale goes—once a Vikings fan, always a Vikings fan.

From tailgating outside Metropolitan Stadium to the time-honored TV footage of flamethrowers vainly attempting to thaw frozen turf for playoff games to the deafening roar of Vikings fans confined under the roof of the Metrodome, Sundays have always been a time when the entire state stops for three hours and pays homage to the Vikings. Whether they warmed your frozen hearts on sub-zero December days or broke them with four Super Bowl losses on late January afternoons, the Vikings have been as much a part of Minnesota as its trademark lakes, bone numbing temperatures and distinct change of seasons.

The cast of characters and chain of events that have solidified the resolve of Vikings fans runs deeply in the minds and hearts of those who have followed the purple and gold since its inaugural season in 1961. From fiery coaches like "The Dutchman" Norm Van Brocklin and lovable vulgarian Jerry Burns to stoic Hall of Famer Bud Grant to self-confident and media-wary Dennis Green, the headmasters of the Vikings have always made sure there was never a dull moment. Fans even remember the malaise year of 1984 when Big Brother, in the form of ex-Vietnam drill sergeant Les Steckel, took the Vikings to the lowest moments in franchise history—one that longtime Vikings fans have compared with the "Dallas" TV series when it turned out an entire season did not exist.

As different and outlandish as the coaches that have led the Vikings were, the players were equally disparate. The quiet drive of Alan Page, the free spiritedness of death-defiant Jim Marshall and the blackboard-breaking competitive spirit of Carl Eller joined to create one of the greatest defensive lines in the history of the NFL—the Purple People Eaters. In later years, the Vikings would come close to recreating those glory days with defensive monsters like Keith Millard, Chris Doleman, Henry Thomas and John Randle.

Could two running backs be more different than Bill Brown and Chuck Foreman? Brown was a player who so loved the game, he would have played not only with a broken leg, but an amputated one. Short, slow and bowlegged, he looked more like a beer vendor than an NFL player, yet still holds the team record for touchdowns with 76 over 13 years. Foreman was a slippery running back with a rare blend of power and speed that, through his receiving ability, revolutionized the position—although NFL historians may not duly credit his role in opening up offenses. What do they have in common? They were both embraced by fans of the Minnesota Vikings and were key reasons why the teams they played on enjoyed success, along with lesser-known players like Dave Osborn, Robert Smith, Ted Brown and Darrin Nelson. They were different backs with different styles, but they shared the adoration as Viking heroes.

How about players like Paul Krause and Cris Carter? Both were picked up off the NFL scrap heap by the Vikings. Krause was viewed as not fast enough, mean enough or big enough to be an effective NFL defensive back. He ended his career as the NFL's all-time leading interceptor, and, in 1998, was elected to the NFL Hall of Fame. Carter was released by the Philadelphia Eagles and former Vikings assistant coach Buddy Ryan because "all he does is catch touchdowns." Once in Minnesota, he became one of the greatest receivers the game has ever seen. He transformed his life from being a wild nightlife partier to being an ordained minister with strong Christian beliefs and, in all likelihood, will eventually join Krause in Canton.

Perhaps the position that best describes the diversity of players that have called the frozen North their home are the quarterbacks that have donned Viking horns. There was the son of a Georgia minister named Francis whose self-confidence turned off some fans and teammates alike, but went on to shatter every existing passing record that stood at the time he played. There was a fiery Chicano named Joe Kapp who had the uniform number of a quarterback, but the mentality of a linebacker and was the catalyst to the Vikings' "40-for-60" NFL championship season of 1969. There was a cocky Texan named Tommy Kramer who convinced his teammates than no deficit couldn't be overcome and just as many bartenders that last call shouldn't apply to a pro athlete. There were great players nearing the end of their careers—Warren Moon looking for his elusive first Super Bowl ring and Jim McMahon looking to recapture some of the glory that made him a champion. And there is Brad Johnson, an "aw, shucks" kind of player who hasn't let the big money of the NFL jade his "Everyman" outlook on life or the game. He has taught players and fans alike that patience and persistence will eventually pay off.

These are just a few of the players that have forged a legacy of Minnesota Vikings football. The Twins have brought world championships back to Minnesota, the Timberwolves show the promise to do so in the near future and the North Stars gave native Minnesotans a hometown professional stage on which to showcase their talents. But no professional team has had the impact on the state that the Minnesota Vikings have. From the time training camp opens in the sweltering temperatures of July until the season ends about 100 degrees or more colder, the Vikings are still the only show in Minnesota.

Whether it's the unending prayers the fans have that eventually the Vikings will finally win the Big One or the shared triumph and pain that the populous has shared as a collective experience, the Vikings are as big a legend in Minnesota as Paul Bunyan and Babe the Blue Ox. This book will hopefully introduce novice Vikings fans to some of the fabled history of the team's early years, those who have lost touch with the Vikings an update as to where their team has come and for longtime fans a chance to reminisce about the team's past and present. Whether through wind-swept Met Stadium or the climate-controlled Metrodome, Minnesotans—natives, transplants and the relocated—still boast "I'm a Viking fan." This book will test your knowledge and maybe open your eyes to something you didn't know about the team that remains the love interest of so many purple-dyed fans.

Fran Tarkenton

1

IN THE BEGINNING

T he creation of the Minnesota Vikings is a story that has largely gone unreported by football historians, but without its bizarre beginning, Minnesota may have never had a future in the league. The fact that the Vikings are still in the NFL is as much a credit to Chicago's fabled George Halas than anyone else, as Halas helped force the NFL to accept Minnesota—more out of self-interest than any sense of good for the league.

In 1959, Max Winter and partners Bill Boyer and H.P. Skoglund made the paltry deposit of $25,000 to secure an AFL franchise—an upstart rival to the established NFL. While most of the AFL's fledgling franchises were located on the east and west coasts, Minnesota's franchise was located in the middle of territory previously held as the exclusive domain of the Chicago Bears and Green Bay Packers.

Sensing the potential for a rival league to steal away some of his fan base to the new league, Halas moved fast. His solution? Make the Vikings an expansion franchise in the NFL. But this spur of the moment solution was far from a done deal. Unlike the inexpensive entry fee to join the AFL, the Minnesota money men were going to have to pony up $1 million—a $600,000 payment up front in 1960 and a $400,000 payment before the team began play in 1961.

Needing to get additional financing, Winter and his group brought St. Paul newspaper magnate Bernie Ridder—of the famed Knight-Ridder newspaper syndicate—on board as a 30 percent owner to provide the financial backing to accommodate the $1 million franchise fee. But the Vikings ordeal wasn't over quite yet. There was going to be one more sticking point—an aging man from Duluth named Ole Haugsrud. Haugsrud was a Duluth businessman who joined the NFL in 1923 as the owner of the Duluth Eskimos. Back in the '20s, just about anyone who could field a team and generate any revenue was accepted into the NFL and Haugsrud was no exception. He bankrolled the Eskimos on the strength of star running back Ernie Nevers, a bull of back who was born in nearby Willow River, and made Nevers the NFL's gate attraction counterpart to the AFL's Red Grange. The Eskimos played almost all of their games on the road and, when Nevers wore down from the strain of being the one-man show, the Eskimos followed—folding up the tents on their traveling circus in 1925.

However, Haugsrud's secession from the NFL was part of an agreement that entitled him to a claim on any NFL franchise if the league ever returned to Minnesota. Haugsrud's approval cost 10 percent of the team's stock, but, with his signature on the franchise agreement, the Vikings were prepared to bring football back to Minnesota and into Metropolitan Stadium.

The initial requirements of a new franchise were to get the personnel in place. The first move in that regard was to hire Bert Rose as the team's general manager. Shortly thereafter, fiery coach Norm Van Brocklin was brought in to evaluate talent and assemble a rag-tag collection of players from other teams' rosters and through the draft.

Although the franchise's first steps were baby steps, Minnesota was in the NFL and ready to begin play in September, 1961.

TRIVIA QUESTIONS

1. The Vikings were not the first NFL team to hail from Minnesota. In fact, since the NFL began keeping records in 1920, the Vikings were the fifth Minnesota franchise. Who were the first four?

2. One of those three teams earned the nickname "Iron Men of the North" for a good reason. Which team was it and why did it earn the nickname?

3. When Ernie Nevers was signed by the Eskimos, what was his salary?

4. When Minnesota was awarded an AFL franchise in 1959, whose brainchild was the rival league?

5. Minnesota was to be one of eight teams in the AFL. What franchises were to compose the original eight AFL teams?

6. When the AFL conducted its first organizational meeting and college draft, where was the meeting held?

7. At that meeting, a college draft was conducted. Who did the Vikings take with their first pick and what made the pick a bit ironic years later?

8. When Minnesota pulled out of the AFL, what franchise took its place?

9. How much did Ole Haugsrud have to pay to buy his 10 percent interest in the team?

10. Who was the first person hired as an employee of the Minnesota Vikings and what was his job?

11. Metropolitan Stadium was not the original home of NFL football in the Twin Cities. At what stadium did the Minneapolis Marines and Red Jackets play their home games?

12. The Vikings didn't play the first regular season NFL game at

Metropolitan Stadium. What teams played that game and what was the final score?

13. In what city was Metropolitan Stadium located?

14. When the franchise was named the Minnesota Vikings, it created a first of its kind in the history of the NFL. What about the name made it so unique?

15. Newly elected NFL Commissioner Pete Rozelle insisted that the Minnesota group pay an up-front cost of $600,000 for its new franchise. What was the purpose of that payment?

16. Before the team could begin play, a site had to be chosen to conduct training camp. What city was selected?

17. Two coaches who went on to become legends in their own right were originally offered the Vikings head coaching job prior to the hiring of Norm Van Brocklin. Who were they and where were they coaching at the time?

18. Prior to coming to the Vikings in 1961, what did Norm Van Brocklin do in 1960 that forever placed him in the annals of NFL lore?

19. Before buying the Vikings, owner Max Winter was the general manager of what professional sports team?

20. What was the name of the Twin Cities-based civic group that helped meet the NFL's demand of 25,000 season tickets prior to the end of the 1961 season opener?

2

THE DUTCHMAN
AND HIS WAYWARD SONS

Norm Van Brocklin was an unlikely selection to be the coach of an expansion team. As a player, he was a fierce competitor who played hard and drank hard. He was accustomed to success—his final game as a professional was to lead the Philadelphia Eagles to the 1960 NFL championship. His arrival to Minnesota would be a rude awakening.

Not exactly familiar with the ways of the expansion world, Van Brocklin was less than enthusiastic about his new charges when the team opened training camp in Bemidji in the summer of '61. It was a cattle call of epic proportions, including players who were at the end of the line, players with criminal records and Minnesotans who held the belief that "they ain't so tough" when they saw NFLers on TV. They all converged—to the Dutchman's dismay.

Van Brocklin came up for a term for his new players picked up in the expansion draft—"36 stiffs." He expected that the team would have a heck of a time winning any games when he first saw the group of sorry outcasts that had been assembled. But his team was not without some star power.

The Vikings had mortgaged the 1962 college draft to bring in Van Brocklin's quarterback of the future from the New York Giants—George Shaw—and an undersized defensive end who would become the game's ultimate iron man—Jim Marshall. There was running back Hugh

McElhenny, who had been a star with the San Francisco 49ers for nine seasons, and a collection of high draft picks that would help mold the Vikings.

In the first round, the Vikings used the first pick in the draft on Tulane running back Tommy Mason, which was followed up by free spirited linebacker Rip Hawkins out of North Carolina. But without question the best pick was a cocky, undersized quarterback out of Georgia taken in the third round that Van Brocklin called "Peach"—the son of a Baptist minister named Francis Asbury Tarkenton. He was expected to be a reserve until he had mastered the game. That would turn out to be only about 15 minutes.

The first opponent for the Vikings—named so because it represented an aggressive warrior with a will to win and tied into Minnesota's Nordic heritage—was a more familiar name on the NFL landscape, the mighty Chicago Bears. The Bears were recognized as one of the titans of the NFL, but the Vikings and Tarkenton proved to be the master in the franchise opener—stunning the Monsters of the Midway with a 37-13 win. The scrambling youngster dissected the Bear defense, completing 17 of 23 passes for 250 yards and four touchdowns—embarrassing George Halas and putting the Vikings on the map.

Van Brocklin's post-game giddiness after the first win was short-lived. The Vikings would lose 11 of their final 13 games, but the team did show a propensity to play up to the best teams in the league. In two games against NFL powerhouse Baltimore, the Vikings got burned on a 52-yard field goal by Steve Myhra in the closing seconds at Memorial Stadium to lose 34-33 and recorded one of their three wins in 1961 with a 28-20 win over the Colts at Met Stadium—remarkable considering the Colts of 1961 had a roster that included Johnny Unitas, Raymond Berry, Lenny Moore, "Big Daddy" Lipscomb, Art Donovan and Gino Marchetti. The Vikings were a long way from prosperity, but they were coming along.

After a disappointing 2-11-1 season in 1962, the Vikings showed signs of life in '63, finishing 2-1-1 in the final four games to end the season with a 5-8-1 record. Following the 1963 season, the Vikings made a decision that would forever change the way the franchise would progress. Bert Rose resigned as general manager and Jim Finks came in. Finks would later build a powerhouse in Chicago and raise New Orleans from franchise mediocrity, but his success began in Minnesota, where the Vikings went 8-5-1 in 1964 (including 3-0-1 in the final four games) to post their first winning record and get Vikings fans excited about the team's future.

By 1965, the Vikings had many of the component parts in place that would lead the team to greatness. Aside from originals Tarkenton and Marshall, the Vikings had Bill Brown, Carl Eller, Gary Larsen, Dave Osborn, Roy Winston, Mick Tingelhoff and Milt Sunde. Yet, the pieces weren't falling into place. The Vikings went 7-7 in 1965 and the strain was beginning to show on Van Brocklin. After being convinced that the Vikings could be conference champions after finishing second in 1964, the Vikings fell into a fourth-place tie in 1965, and following a humiliating 41-21 loss to the Colts Nov. 14, the Dutchman quit—only to return a day later.

But the moment signaled a change between Van Brocklin and his players. Many felt betrayed that the coach would take such an action, a seeming indictment of his own players. The team wasn't the same. The Vikings limped to a 4-9-1 record in 1966, and after a 41-28 loss to Chicago to end the 1966 season, change was in the air. Van Brocklin and Tarkenton were at each other's throats and both wanted a change. Both announced their retirement as a way to get out of Minnesota. Van Brocklin would resurface as a head coach in Atlanta and Tarkenton used the retirement ploy as a way to force a trade to the Giants.

It seemed that, after a brief glimmer of promise, the Vikings were again on the outs and not in the class of the NFL elite. It was time for Max Winter to again call his friend who had turned down his offer to be the Vikings' first head coach. He again contacted Bud Grant and this time Grant accepted.

TRIVIA QUESTIONS

1. In the expansion draft in which of the Vikings were able to cull players for their own roster, how many of the existing teams' 38 players were owners allowed to protect?

2. While Hugh McElhenny was the best known player taken in the expansion draft, which longtime Viking was plucked off the Detroit Lions roster?

3. McElhenny came to the Vikings with a laudatory nickname. What was it?

4. McElhenny was by far the highest paid Viking of the time. What was his salary in 1961?

5. When the Vikings began play, they were assigned to the Western Conference. What teams comprised the Western Conference that year?

6. The first pre-season game in franchise history was played where and against whom?

7. The first Vikings game at Metropolitan Stadium was the final pre-season game of 1961. Who was the opponent?

8. What was the original seating capacity at Metropolitan Stadium?

9. For years, players and coaches complained that Met Stadium was not a football stadium. What unique quirk specific only to the Met among NFL stadiums made that point painfully evident?

10. Who comprised the starting backfield for the Vikings in their inaugural season opener?

11. The Vikings later earned a notorious reputation for trading away No. 1 draft picks. When was the first time the Vikings traded away a top pick?

12. Who caught Fran Tarkenton's first touchdown pass?

13. Who accounted for the first points scored by the Vikings?

14. Who were the first players named captains of the Vikings?

15. In the first season, two Vikings were named to the Pro Bowl. Who were they?

16. Tommy Mason was a well-known bachelor in the Twin Cities during his playing days. He later married another famous athlete. Who was she?

17. What was Fran Tarkenton's rookie salary?

18. Back in an era of colorful nicknames, running backs Phil King and Bill Brown each had one. What were they?

19. During the early years of the Vikings, where did the team practice?

20. Who was named the first team M.V.P. in 1961?

21. Who was the first Viking to rush for 100 yards?

22. Although known as an iron man in his own right, Tarkenton missed the final game of the 1963 season against the Eagles. Who started in his place?

23. It took three seasons for a Viking to named a consensus All-Pro selection. Who was that player?

24. In 1963, a fourth-round draft pick of the Vikings was named Rookie of the Year—one of only two Vikings ever given the honor. Who was that player and the player who won it a decade later?

25. What player tied an NFL record by recovering eight of his own team's fumbles in 1963?

26. That same season, another Viking set an NFL record for opponent

fumble recoveries with nine. Who was he?

27. As long as we're on the subject of fumble recoveries, two Vikings rank in the top three on the all-time list for fumble recoveries. Who are they and who is the player in second place?

28. Original Viking Paul Dickson was known as a thinking man's player. What was his nickname?

29. Kicker Fred Cox came to the Vikings in 1963. What position did he play at the University of Pittsburgh?

30. Cox ended up making much more money outside of football, as he and a friend patented an item that went on to sell in the millions. What is Cox's unknown claim to fame?

31. When Jim Finks was hired in 1964, what was his previous job?

32. On Aug. 20, 1965, new seats at Met Stadium were dedicated. What was the new seating capacity?

33. In December of the 1966 season, the NFL announced that the two conferences would be split into divisions. What teams were in the Vikings' division?

34. Following the 1966 season, Van Brocklin resigned as head coach. What was his final career record with the Vikings?

35. After the 1966 season, Fran Tarkenton was traded to the Giants for a first- and second-round pick in 1967, a first-round pick in 1968 and a second-round pick in 1969. Who did those choices end up being?

36. What was noteworthy about the 1968 first-round pick?

37. The Bud Grant era began with his hiring on what date?

3

THIS BUD'S FOR YOU

I n the spring of 1967, the Minnesota Vikings made Bud Grant their head coach—a decision that has gone down as one of the greatest personnel moves the team ever made. After turning down the opportunity to coach the Vikings when Max Winter came calling with his expansion invitation, instead opting to remain in the Canadian Football League, Grant became one of the greatest head coaches the NFL has ever seen, winning 158 games—No. 8 all-time and making Grant the only coach in league history to win more than 150 games in less than 20 seasons.

His start in the NFL was a rocky one. The Vikings lost their first four games in 1967 and finished that season with a hideous 3-8-3 record. But Grant was planting the seeds to success in those teams and went on to make the Vikings one of the most dominant teams in the history of the NFL. Fans knew that when playoff time rolled around, the Minnesota Vikings would be in the mix and looking for a Super Bowl title.

While that Super Bowl championship proved elusive, a world title was about all the wasn't within Grant's grasp. In 18 seasons as the head coach of the Vikings, Grant won 15 championships—11 Central Division titles, one NFL championship and three NFC championships. In all, he brought his Vikings to the playoffs 12 times and became a coaching legend in the process.

While known for his unflappable demeanor, Grant was in fact a jovial character who belied his stony sideline facade. He did smile—often in fact—and earned the respect of his players, the fans and the opposition alike. Grant's love of the outdoors became legendary and is something that still keeps his name in the Minnesota media—as a champion of outdoorsmen's rights. On autumn game days, Grant was up at the crack of dawn, not going over opponent tendencies or his own game plan, but instead sitting in a duck blind looking for an elusive mallard or two. His outdoorsman spirit is still evident at the Vikings training facility at Winter Park in Eden Prairie, Minn. Grant installed a deer feeder on the site and, in the late afternoon, deer still frequent the lush grass of the Vikings outdoor training field for a snack.

When he was inducted into the NFL Hall of Fame in 1994, he gave an emotional speech that finally let the world see a side of Bud Grant that had been hidden before—that of a man with the ability to get choked up, teary-eyed and show emotion. While his players had seen that before, the Grant stereotype of being a stoic man behind steely eyes was an image that Grant didn't mind being promoted. Never one to seek the spotlight, Grant was a general, a leader. But in that misty-eyed moment at his induction ceremony, Grant paid a tribute to his father, looking skyward and saying, "The kid finally made it."

For those who followed Grant's coaching career over the years, they knew Grant made it long before his induction into the Hall of Fame—even without a world championship ring on his finger.

TRIVIA QUESTIONS

1. In what town was Bud Grant born?

2. Where did Grant attend college?

3. In his college career, Grant earned nine varsity letters. In what sports did he participate and get his letters?

4. Grant's real name isn't "Bud." What is his full given name?

5. Before coming to the NFL, Grant coached 10 years in the Canadian Football League. What team did he coach?

6. In his 10 years in the CFL, how many Grey Cup championships did he win?

7. In Grant's first season as Vikings coach in 1967, Fran Tarkenton had left the team. Who was his incumbent starting quarterback that season?

8. A stickler for respect and attention, Grant insisted his players stand in perfect formation during the playing of the National Anthem. What player did he first put in charge of this ritual—a duty he maintained for a decade?

9. When Grant came out of college, he was sought after in two professional sports. What two were they?

10. What sport did Grant originally choose and who was the team and coach he played for in 1950?

11. Despite not playing in the NFL in 1950, Grant was the first round pick of what team?

12. In 1952, Grant had a season worthy of the Pro Bowl. At what position did he play and what numbers did he post in his only season of full-time duty in the NFL?

13. What was Grant's final record as an NFL head coach?

14. Of head coaches with 15 or more years at the helm, only four coaches had a better career winning percentage than Grant's 62 percent efficiency. Can you name those four coaches?

15. When Grant was voted into the Hall of Fame in 1994, he was one of six members inducted, including three who once played for the Dallas Cowboys. Can you name the Hall of Fame Class of 1994 that joined Grant?

4

THE GLORY YEARS

T he Bud Grant era with the Vikings got off to a sluggish start, as the Vikings struggled without Fran Tarkenton and were only beginning to reap the harvest of the trade that sent him to the Giants. The Vikings lost their first four games that season, but won the first game under Grant against a team that would become one of their great rivals through his tenure—a 10-7 win over the defending and eventual repeating Super Bowl champion Green Bay Packers. That win would be one of the few blemishes on Vince Lombardi's record in 1967, but served as a portent of things to come—the Vikings would later lose a 30-27 nail-biter late in the season to the Packers.

The 1967 season proved to Grant and the Vikings that the team wasn't far away from being a contender—despite a horrendous 3-8-3 record. Aside from the three ties, four of the Vikings' eight losses were by five points or less and the team was preparing to get a big boost in the way of solid draft choices that would help build the Vikings into a perennial Central Division champion.

The pieces began falling into place in '67, when the Vikings had an unprecedented three first-round draft picks, acquired by general manager-extraordinaire Jim Finks. The first pick came from the Tarkenton trade and was used on running back Clinton Jones, who would serve as an excellent complement to the bruising styles of Bill Brown and Dave Osborn. The second pick was the Vikings' own and it was used on gliding wide receiver

Gene Washington, who became a potent weapon in stretching opposing defenses. But the third first-rounder would be truly special.

Acquired in a trade with the Los Angeles Rams and quite likely the difference between the Vikings going to four Super Bowls and the Rams going to only one was Notre Dame defensive tackle Alan Page. With speed unseen before among defensive linemen, Page became one of the dominant forces in the NFL. If Page had not been a member of the Purple People Eaters and was instead another link in the Fearsome Foursome with Deacon Jones and Merlin Olsen, the balance of power could easily have shifted away from the Vikings in later years. But Page was a Viking and one of the key reasons the Viking defense became one of the best in the history of the NFL.

The Vikings weren't done reaping a draft harvest. The team picked up a speedy defensive back named Bobby Bryant late in the 1967 draft and added perennial All-Pro Ron Yary and cornerback Charlie West in the draft of 1968, setting the stage for a series of divisional titles that would have made several Vikings Hall of Famers had one season ended with a Super Bowl championship.

The Vikings didn't set the league on fire in 1968, losing three straight games in October and two more late in the season. But, thanks to a down year in the NFC Central, the Vikings won their first division title with an 8-6 record—winning road games at San Francisco and Philadelphia to close the season and send the Vikings to the playoffs for the first time in team history. Following the win over the Eagles, the Vikings huddled around radios in the locker room to see if the Packers could beat the Bears to give the division title to the Vikes. The Pack obliged with a 28-17 win and the Vikings would make their first appearance in the post-season.

That first playoff appearance was a mere cup of coffee. Traveling to a rainy and windswept Memorial Stadium to play the Colts, the game was scoreless until the final minute of the first half, when Earl Morrall drove the Colts 75 yards for a touchdown. But the game was blown open in the third quarter, as the Colts scored twice in two minutes to take a 21-0 lead. Quarterback Joe Kapp, who had taken over as Tarkenton's replacement during the 1967 season, threw a pair of touchdown passes in the second half, but the Vikings never got closer than 10 points in a 24-14 loss.

But that loss set the stage for possibly the greatest season in Viking history. Lifted by the ability to dominate, the Vikings came together in 1969 (the NFL's 50th anniversary season) behind a slogan created by

Kapp—"40 for 60." The phrase was really quite simple—40 men playing together for 60 minutes can't lose. The Vikings proved that to almost be true. The season opened with disappointment, as the Vikings blew a 17-3 halftime lead to lose to Tarkenton's Giants 24-23. But after that, the Vikings were as dominant as any team in NFL history—including the undefeated 1973 Dolphins and Da Bears of 1985.

Over the final 13 games, no opponent scored more than 14 points on the Vikings. Of those, nine were limited to 10 points or less and six were held to seven points or less. The Vikings' average of 9.5 points a game allowed were the lowest since World War II and the Vikes weren't playing a soft schedule. In 1968, four teams won 10 or more games in the NFL. The Vikings beat three of them—Baltimore, Los Angeles and Cleveland—in 1969 and had to beat the Browns and Rams twice to win the NFL title.

The Vikings shredded teams on both sides of the ball, watching records drop in the process. In Week 2, Kapp tied an NFL record with seven touchdown passes in a 52-14 thrashing of the Colts. In Week 3, the Vikings sacked Bart Starr eight times to improve to 2-1. Four weeks later, Chicago's Bobby Douglass was sacked nine times in 31-14 win that improved the Vikings to 6-1. Next came Cleveland, where the Vikings scored on their first nine possessions on their way to a 51-3 win. But the Vikings still weren't the best of the NFL at that point.

In Week 12, the Vikings had won 10 straight games, but the Rams had started 11-0 as the two teams met for a showdown in L.A. The Vikings took control early and led the entire game—beating the Rams 20-13 and, with a win over the 49ers the next week, the Vikes' 12-game winning streak was the NFL's longest in 35 years. Only a 10-3 loss in a mud bog in Atlanta in the season finale when Grant was resting many of his starters prevented the Vikings from winning 13 straight, but the "40-for-60" juggernaut would not be stopped ... until the Super Bowl.

The Vikings nearly fell off the wagon in the first playoff game, trailing the Rams, 17-7, at halftime. But Minnesota rallied in the second half, highlighted by a sack of Roman Gabriel by Carl Eller for a safety and an interception by Page in the final minutes to preserve a 23-20 win. The Vikings then bounced the Browns, 27-7, to reach their first Super Bowl.

That day would live in infamy for Vikings fans. The Vikings changed up their defense to attack the upstart Kansas City Chiefs. Instead of being the aggressors, the Vikings looked like so many of the victims that they had claimed over the season. Minnesota committed five turnovers and fell behind, 16-0, at halftime, on its way to a 23-7 loss. Much like the Buffalo Bills that would come later, that first loss seemed to have a haunting effect on the Vikings.

The Vikings would continue to be dominant in 1970-71, but had little to show for their efforts. The Vikings won 10 of their last 11 games in 1970 and held opponents to 14 or fewer points in 11 games that season. In 1971, the Vikings won their fourth straight division title and held 12 of 14 opponents to 13 points or less. However, both years the Vikings wound up earning home field—only to lose both times.

In 1970, it was the 49ers that upset the Vikings. Four Viking turnovers and a pair of long punt returns by Bruce Taylor helped John Brodie convert all 17 of San Francisco's points in a 17-14 win. In 1971, it was Dallas that used five turnovers for a 20-12 win over the Vikings.

In the analysis following the 1971 season, it was obvious what the problem was. In three years, the Vikings had compiled a record of 35-7, but had no Super Bowl ring to show for it. The overriding feeling was that, despite a defense that could stifle anybody, the Vikings hadn't been a dominant force since Kapp had left following a contract dispute before the 1970 season. The Vikings had tried and failed using three quarterbacks during that period—Gary Cuozzo, Bob Lee and veteran Norm Snead—but none had been an effective leader. The Vikings needed a quarterback that could get them back to the big game. So a call was made to a disgruntled quarterback that wanted to come to Minnesota. That call was to Fran Tarkenton and, by the 1972 season, Sir Francis was back in purple and gold—ready to bring Minnesota back to the Super Bowl.

Tarkenton's first year with the Vikings didn't live up to the savior status everyone in Minnesota thought it would bring, as the Vikings limped their way to a 7-7 record and lost the division title to Dan Devine's Green Bay Packers. The Vikings lost four of their first six games and, after seemingly getting untracked with a four-game winning streak in October and November, Minnesota lost its last two games to finish out of the playoffs for the first time in five years. It would be five more years before that would happen again.

The Vikings continued to add component pieces to an already strong nucleus. After two seasons of developing few impact players, the Vikings used the 1972 and 1973 drafts to complete the pieces of the puzzle that would get them back to the Super Bowl. In 1972, the Vikings picked up Stanford linebacker Jeff Siemon, who would become the force the Vikings needed in the middle of the defense. In 1973, the Vikings retooled the backfield, using their first pick to select running back Chuck Foreman, a back who helped revolutionize the game as a runner and receiver. In addition, the Vikes added key role players in cornerback Jackie Wallace, wide receiver Jim Lash and running back Brent McClanahan.

As the 1973 season opened, the Vikings had Tarkenton at quarterback, Foreman, Bill Brown, Dave Osborn and McClanahan in the backfield, John Gilliam as the go-to receiver, Grady Alderman, Ron Yary, Mick Tingelhoff, Ed White and Milt Sunde on the offensive line, Page, Eller, Jim Marshall and Gary Larsen on the defensive front, Siemon, Roy Winston and Wally Hilgenberg at linebacker, Paul Krause, Bryant, Nate Wright and Jeff Wright in the defensive backfield and Fred Cox doing the kicking. There wasn't a weakness on the team and the Vikings played that way.

The season started like no other in Viking history. The Vikings won all five of their pre-season games and went on to win their first nine games of the regular season—clinching the Central Division before losing a game when the team beat Detroit, 28-7, on November 11. With the exception of a couple of blips on the screen—losses to sub-par Atlanta and Cincinnati—the Vikings were as dominant as ever, scoring 22 or more points in nine games while holding opponents to single digits in an amazing seven games.

The Vikings nearly saw another tremendous season squandered in the playoffs, but their first-round game against the Redskins became the making of a legend. Trailing, 7-3, at halftime of a lethargic playoff game, Eller decided it was time to motivate his teammates. He did so by taking his heavily taped fist and smashing it into a blackboard in the locker room. The result? The blackboard shattered and Eller scared his teammates into one of the best halves of post-season football the Vikings ever played. The Vikings drove 75 yards on the first series of the second half to take the lead and, following a pair of field goals by Washington, Tarkenton and Gilliam hooked up twice for touchdowns and a 27-20 win.

Next came Dallas and the Vikings weren't about to let playoff history be repeated. Having to travel to Texas Stadium, the Vikings were never seriously challenged. The team ran for 203 yards against the Bob Lilly-less Cowboys and, if not for a 63-yard punt return by Golden Richards, the Vikings would have caned the Cowboys even worse than the 27-10 final would indicate. The Vikings were heading back to the Big Show, but, once again, the result would be the same.

The Miami Dolphins crushed the Vikings early, scoring on their first two drives and limiting the Viking offense to only seven plays in the first quarter to take a 14-0 lead. The Vikings' only chance to get back in the game came late in the first half when they drove to the Miami 6-yard line. But a critical fumble kept Miami in control of momentum and Larry Csonka had a Super Bowl-record day on the ground, helping the Dolphins cruise to a second straight title with a 24-7 win.

Undaunted by their previous lack of success, the Vikings were back to the Super Bowl in 1974, but the cast was beginning to change. The biggest change in the historical perspective was that Finks left the Vikings. In contract negotiations, Finks, a respected football man who was later enshrined in the NFL Hall of Fame, wanted ownership of team stock as part of his next contract. To the surprise of many, he was denied by Max Winter and left. The man who took his place became an infamous part of Viking history—Memphis millionaire Mike Lynn. Although he wasn't immediately made the general manager, he was the assistant to the declining Winter, Lynn essentially oversaw every aspect of the team operation. He specialized in contract negotiation, which at the time was specializing in putting a gun to a player's head.

The 1974 Vikings were well entrenched with star players and got a talent infusion with the addition of rookie linebackers Fred McNeill and Matt Blair. The Vikings were starting to show the signs of age, but still had the horses to be dominant. The Vikings won their first five games and their last three to finish the season 10-4 and play host during the playoffs.

The Vikings used a pair of turnovers to break open a 7-7 halftime tie with the St. Louis Cardinals to score 16 third-quarter points on their way to a 30-14 win. Foreman continued to impress, gaining 114 yards on the ground and Tarkenton hooked up with Gilliam for a back-breaking 38-yard touchdown. The Vikings and Rams played another championship game classic on December 29, as the Viking defense came up big when it had to. The Rams gained 340 yards against the Vikings, but managed only one touchdown—that late in the game with the Vikings ahead, 14-3. For a second straight year the Vikings were going to the Super Bowl. But this time it wasn't against the former Dolphin dynasty. It was against an emerging dynasty—the Pittsburgh Steelers.

If you ask Vikings players, the Steelers were the team the Vikings had the best shot at beating of all the Super Bowl losses. The game was a defensive struggle, with the only points of the first half coming on a safety.

The game swung in Pittsburgh's direction on a Viking fumble on the opening kickoff of the second half and the Steelers recovered on the Minnesota 30—driving for a touchdown. The Vikings still had a chance late in the game, when the Vikings blocked a Pittsburgh punt for a touchdown, but Cox shanked the extra point to keep the score, 9-6. On the next drive, with four minutes to play, Minnesota appeared to knock the ball loose from Franco Harris, an apparent fumble recovered by the Vikings. The referees ruled Harris was down and the Steelers drove the length of the field for the game-clinching touchdown. Harris had another record-setting day against the Vikings defense, while Minnesota's offense was limited to only 119 yards by the Steel Curtain—putting the Vikings at 0-3 in Super Bowl competition.

Viking purists believe the best team of all may have been the 1975 squad. Tarkenton had an MVP season, and the team started 10-0, winning nine games by 10 or more points. The Vikings outscored their opponents, 377-180, and were primed to make a return to the Super Bowl. That was, until the Dallas Cowboys created one of the most famous plays in the history of the NFL.

There are plays that will forever be linked with a team and an era. There was the finish to "The Ice Bowl" game in Green Bay, "The Immaculate Reception" by Harris, "The Catch" by Dwight Clark off the arm of Joe Montana and the Raiders' improbable "Holy Roller" play. But no play has been so reviewed or become as big a part of the NFL vocabulary as the "Hail Mary."

The Vikings forced the Cowboys to come to the Met for a frosty game, which looked to swing the Vikes' way early, as McNeill recovered a muffed punt on the Dallas 1-yard line, where Foreman took it in for a score. The defenses dominated the game, but, with 5:24 to play, McClanahan scored on a 1-yard run to cap a 70-yard drive to give the Vikings a 14-10 lead. Roger Staubach refused to give up, however, and needed to drive Dallas 85 yards. The Vikings forced him to throw short and eat up precious clock time, but, with 24 seconds left from the 50-yard line, Staubach heaved the infamous Hail Mary. Drew Pearson pushed off of Nate Wright and hauled in the pass, looking for penalty flags on the play that never came. The stunned crowd of 46,425 fell silent as the Cowboys crushed the Vikings dream season and went on to represent the NFC in the Super Bowl.

With an aging cast of players, the Vikings knew that the 1976 season could well be the last chance the team had to make a run at the Super Bowl.

Key players like Tarkenton, Eller, Tingelhoff, Hilgenberg and Krause were showing the signs of age. This would be the last stand for the glory days of the Vikings—a team growing old together. They played with a sense of urgency and gave the fans one last wild ride to the Super Bowl.

The defense never let up, allowing only three teams to score more than 13 points and new receiving targets—rookie Sammy White and veteran Ahmad Rashad—gave the Vikings a one-two punch offensively to go with Foreman. The Vikings didn't lose a game until Halloween and wrapped up their eighth division title in nine years on November 21 with a 17-10 win against Green Bay. For a team that let everything hang out for what many conceded was the last legitimate shot at the Super Bowl ring, the Vikings had the best record in the NFC and needed to show it in the playoffs to get another shot at a championship.

The Vikings thrashed Washington in the opening round, building a lead, 35-6, after three quarters and coasting to a 35-20 win, setting up another championship battle with the Rams to determine the NFC champion.

The championship game helped stamp Bobby Bryant's mark on team history. The expected defensive battle materialized and the Rams refused to go for a touchdown on a fourth-and-goal from the Vikings 1-yard line. Settling for a field goal, Nate Wright came through and blocked the kick, which Bryant scooped up on the 10-yard line and raced 90 yards for a score. The Vikings would take a 17-0 lead before the Rams rallied for two scores to cut the Vikings lead to 17-13—thanks to a blocked extra point. Forced to go for a touchdown trailing by four, the Rams were stopped twice in Viking territory in the fourth quarter and reserve running back Sammy Johnson scored the final touchdown to give the Vikes a 24-13 win and send them back for a fourth shot at a Super Bowl title against the perennial AFC playoff bridesmaid—the Oakland Raiders.

The Raiders hammered the Vikings from start to finish, building a 16-0 halftime lead that became 19-0 early in the third quarter. The swagger was gone from the Vikings and the Raiders never let up, piling up a Super Bowl-record 429 yards on offense and scoring a clinching touchdown on a 75-yard interception return by Willie Brown for a 32-14 crushing of the Vikes.

At the end of that game, it was painfully evident that the glory years of the Vikings were over. Four Super Bowl losses—each seemingly more humiliating than the last—proved too much. It was obvious things were going to change and key personnel was going to need to be replaced

—starting with Tarkenton. When the Vikings used their first pick of the 1977 draft to take quarterback Tommy Kramer, the handwriting was on the wall. It was a great run, but it was over.

TRIVIA QUESTIONS

1. Gary Larsen was the least-known member of the Purple People Eaters defensive front during the Viking glory years. How was he obtained?

2. When the Vikings acquired quarterback Gary Cuozzo to be Fran Tarkenton's replacement, who did they make the trade with and what did they give up?

3. In the 1968 season, when the Vikings won their first NFC Central Division title, what was their longest winning streak of that season?

4. Who scored the Vikings' first post-season touchdown?

5. Following the Vikings' 1968 playoff loss to Baltimore, they played another game—against the loser of the other NFL conference championship game. What was the name of this ill-fated, meaningless game?

6. In that game, who did the Vikings play, what was the outcome and where was it played?

7. Who started at quarterback in the season opener of the 1969 season?

8. In Week 2 of the 1969 season, Joe Kapp threw seven touchdown passes. Who were on the receiving end of those NFL-record passes?

9. What national political figure was in the stands during that 7-TD game vs. Baltimore?

10. In a Week 3 home game against the Green Bay Packers October 5, 1969, the Vikings made history for two reasons in relation to the game

site. What were the two noteworthy aspects of that game?

11. Joe Kapp was the consummate team player—even when it came to signing autographs. How would Kapp sign an autograph during the 1969 season?

12. Following a 12-game winning streak in 1969, the Vikings lost the regular-season finale, 10-3, to Atlanta. What was noteworthy about that game?

13. Kapp was given the team M.V.P. award in the 1969 season, but turned it down. Why?

14. In the 1969 divisional playoffs against the Rams, what player scored two touchdowns?

15. Who became the first Vikings player to rush for 100 yards in a playoff game—the 27-7 win over Cleveland in the 1969 NFL title game?

16. In that win over the Browns, Joe Kapp completed a 75-yard touchdown pass to what receiver?

17. While the Super Bowl appearance at the end of the 1969 season was a first for the Vikings, it wasn't for a Viking assistant coach. It was his third in four Super Bowls. Who was he?

18. What was memorable about Joe Kapp's Viking career after the Super Bowl loss to the Chiefs?

19. Who was the first regular-season opponent of the Vikings following the Super Bowl loss in January 1970?

20. What two teams beat the Vikings in the 1970 regular season?

21. In the 1970 playoff loss to the 49ers, the Vikings led only once, following this player's touchdown. Who scored that touchdown in the first quarter to give the Vikings a 7-0 lead?

22. During the Vikings run for the title from 1969 to 1971, Fred Cox set an NFL record for consecutive games with at least one field goal. In how many consecutive games did Cox hit a field goal?

23. Who was named team M.V.P. in 1970 and what made the honor one that he was worthy of?

24. In 1971, the Vikings rush defense tied a record set by the 1934 Lions and 1968 Cowboys. What incredible record did the Vikes tie?

25. During the Vikings glory years, the team lost only two games in five different seasons. What seasons were they?

26. On December 12, 1969, the Viking defense set a team record against the 49ers. What was that record?

27. In the 1970 season, how many passing touchdowns did the Viking defense allow?

28. From 1969 to 1971, the Vikings led the NFL in one important category each season. What category was it?

29. The last two wins of the 1970 season over Boston and Atlanta were memorable in what respect?

30. Who started the 1971 playoff loss to Dallas?

31. How did the Vikings score their 12 points in that game?

32. In 1972, the Vikings traded to get Fran Tarkenton back. What did the Vikings give up to get him back from the Giants?

33. What was Tarkenton's salary in 1972?

34. Three Vikings negotiated their contracts as a group in 1972. Who were those players and what eventually happened to them?

35. What was the Vikings' record against playoff-bound teams in 1972?

36. Including pre-season, how many consecutive games did the Vikings win to start the 1973 season?

37. What former professional wrestler predicted the Vikings would lose, 27-0, to Cincinnati before the December 2, 1973 game?

38. That shutout to Cincinnati broke a string of how many games in which the Vikings had not been shut out?

39. How many games would pass before the Vikings were shut out again and what made that shutout somewhat ironic?

40. From the start of the 1969 season through the end of 1976 when the Vikings gave up 32 points to the Raiders, how many teams scored more than 24 points—post-season and regular-season—in that span of 124 games?

41. In the 1973 regular-season finale against the New York Giants, where was the game played? Hint: It was the Giants' home in 1973 and 1974.

42. In the infamous Carl Eller "blackboard-busting" game, who caught two fourth-quarter touchdown passes to solidify the win?

43. What was unique about the Vikings' 27-10 win in the 1973 NFC Championship over Dallas?

44. How many times was Alan Page named NFC Defensive Player of the Year?

45. From September 15, 1968 to September 15, 1974, Fred Cox had a record number of consecutive extra-point kicks that started and ended on the same date. How many extra points did Cox make in a row between misses?

46. Who was Cox's holder for almost all of his Vikings career?

47. In 1974, Mike Lynn was hired by Max Winter as his personal

administrative assistant following the resignation of Jim Finks. How did Lynn come to the attention of the NFL?

48. At the start of the 1974 season, the Vikings scored only seven points in a game at Detroit and 11 points in a home game the next week against the Bears. What was noteworthy about those two consecutive games?

49. Twice during the 1974 season, the Vikings lost back-to-back games. Prior to that, the last time the Vikings lost three games in a row was in October 1968. When was the next time the Vikings would go on a three-game losing streak?

50. In the Vikings' 30-14 playoff win over St. Louis, what player scored two touchdowns?

51. In the Vikings' 14-10 win over the Rams in the 1974 NFC Championship Game, who scored Minnesota's two touchdowns?

52. The four-point title win by the Vikings was the narrowest margin of victory since a 17-16 win in the 1953 NFL title game. What two teams played in that game?

53. Some would argue that the Vikings team of 1975 was the greatest in team history. How many Vikings made the Pro Bowl in 1975 and can you name them?

54. In only two subsequent seasons—even after the advent of the 16-game schedule—did a Vikings team score more points than the 1975 team did. How many points did the Vikings score in 1975?

55. How many games in a row did the Vikings win to start the 1975 season?

56. What team finally ended the Vikings' perfect season in 1975?

57. The "Hail Mary" playoff game against Dallas was one of the low points in Viking history. One fan got his own retribution by hitting the back judge who didn't make the pass interference call so many thought

should have been made in the head with a Jack Daniels bottle. Who was that referee?

58. In March, 1976, one of the team's founding ownership members died. Which one was it?

59. In the first seven games of the 1976 season, the Vikings went 6-0-1. How many total points did the Vikings allow in those seven games?

60. From 1969 to 1976, the Vikings played 56 regular-season games at Met Stadium. What was their record during that span?

61. The Vikings were a model of consistency during the latter part of the glory years. It was earlier asked how long the Vikings went without losing three straight games following back-to-back losses in November, 1974. How many games did the Vikings play before they lost even two straight?

62. The Vikings were notorious fast starters during the Super Bowl years of 1969-76. What was the team's September record in the 21 games it played during those years?

63. Just as impressive was the team's record in December during those years, despite often resting key starters down the stretch to avoid injuries. In the 22 games played in December during those years, what was the Vikings' record?

64. In the playoffs following the 1997 season, two running backs for the eventual champion Denver Broncos—Terrell Davis and Derek Loville— each ran for 100 yards. Prior to that, the last time it had been done in a playoff game by two players from the same team was in the 1976 playoffs when the Vikings beat Washington 35-20 at the Met. Who were the two running backs that both went over the century mark?

65. In that same game, Fran Tarkenton became the first Viking quarterback to throw three touchdowns in a playoff game. Who were on the receiving end of those passes?

66. The key to the Vikings' final NFC Championship win during the Purple Power Years was a 90-yard blocked field goal return by Bobby Bryant. From 1969 to 1976, the Vikings played 11 NFC playoff games. In how many of those games did the defense or special teams score and what was the Vikings' record in those games?

Hall of Fame quarterback Fran Tarkenton completes a pass against the Green Bay Packers at Milwaukee County Stadium.

5

CLOSE BUT NO CIGAR

L ong before Denver, and later Buffalo, wore the big slobbering monkey on their backs for "not being able to win the big one," it was a title the Vikings teams wore with sadness. As overpowering as many of those teams were against divisional opponents and NFC playoff foes, once the Vikings got to the Super Bowl, their fortress crumbled and the team fell flat and hard.

It started with Kansas City, when Bud Grant made one of the few coaching blunders of his career. Having heard *ad nauseam* about the Chiefs' "new offense" that was going to revolutionize football, the coaching staff changed a game plan that was one of the most effective in NFL history during the 1969 season. The result? The Vikings would be dazed, confused and humbled by the Chiefs—giving further legitimacy to the AFL only a year after Joe Namath made his brash predictions that the brand of ball in the AFL was equal to that in the established NFL.

After failing to get back over the next three years and assigning much of the blame for that to instability at quarterback, the Vikings made the moves to get Fran Tarkenton back and expected that he would be the southern general that would lead the Vikings to the nirvana of the NFL and make Bloomington "Title Town West." Instead, with many players at the peak of their abilities, the result was the same, as the Vikings would qualify for the Super Bowl three times in four years only to be denied—soundly —on all three occasions.

First came Miami. History recalls the Dolphins of the early 1970s as one of the greatest teams of all time. With a no-name defense and a bruising running back named Larry Csonka, the Dolphins ran over, around and through the Vikings for a humiliating 24-7 caning.

Next came the Steelers. Again, the Vikings would run into a team that was going to be remembered prominently in discussions of the greatest teams of all time. With Terry Bradshaw, Franco Harris and the Steel Curtain in their prime, the Steelers helped earn their status as Team of the Decade with a hard-fought defensive battle and a 16-6 win in a game that wasn't decided until the final five minutes. That game helped put a sharper focus on the Vikings' problems in the Super Bowl. The Chiefs, many theorized, was a fluke. The Dolphins, many conceded, were one of the greatest teams ever—by any standards. But the Steelers didn't have the Vikings' Super Bowl experience and didn't—at the time, anyway—have the recognized stars that Minnesota had. That loss was a knife in the chest of the organization.

Then following a loss to the Cowboys in the 1975 playoffs—a year when the Vikings were convinced there was no team in the NFL that could touch them—the Vikings got a fourth shot at glory against the Oakland Raiders. At the time, the Raiders held the stigma of a big-game loser—annually making the playoffs, but never making the Super Bowl. A team that in many ways mirrored the Vikings—a core of star players aging together—the Raiders hammered the Vikings like no other Super Bowl opponent had. The annihilation was complete—offensively, defensively and on special teams. It was perhaps the organization's darkest hour.

Since then, the Vikings have never returned to the Super Bowl and so many of those talented players of that era retired from the game begging for one more chance to redeem themselves. Were the Vikings losers? The record books say yes. The fans who lived through the glorious runs to those losses say no. But those two opposing viewpoints will never meet. The only thing that can be agreed upon is that neither Viking fans nor their detractors would be in serious disagreement had the Vikings won just one of those games—and probably at least a handful more Vikings from that era would have their busts on display in the NFL Hall of Fame in Canton.

But, those four Sundays were anything but Super for the Vikings.

TRIVIA QUESTIONS

1. For the record, what Super Bowls did the Vikings play in?

2. In what city and stadium was the Super Bowl against Kansas City played?

3. In what city and stadium was the Super Bowl against Miami played?

4. In what city and stadium was the Super Bowl against Pittsburgh played?

5. In what city and stadium was the Super Bowl against Oakland played?

6. What attendance-related record was set in the Vikings' last Super Bowl appearance?

7. What two teams did the Vikings beat following the 1969 season to win the NFL Championship and make the Super Bowl?

8. What two teams did Kansas City beat following the 1969 season to win the AFL Championship and make the Super Bowl?

9. How many points were the Vikings favored to win by in Super Bowl IV?

10. Who accounted for Kansas City's first three scores of the game?

11. The turning point of the game came on a second-quarter kickoff return fumble. What Viking fumbled the ball and what Chief recovered the fumble?

12. Who converted that turnover into a touchdown to give the Chiefs a 16-0 halftime lead?

13. Who scored the Vikings' only touchdown of Super Bowl IV and how

did it happen?   .

14. On the next drive, the Chiefs salted the game away when quarterback Len Dawson threw a short pass that turned into a 46-yard touchdown. Who caught the pass and what Viking did he burn to get free for the long score?

15. In the fourth quarter of that game, Joe Kapp and his late replacement Gary Cuozzo were intercepted three times. What Chief defenders made those interceptions?

16. Mike Garrett was the game's leading rusher. How many yards did he gain against the Viking defense?

17. Who was the Vikings' leader rusher and how many yards did he gain?

18. In that game, one Viking had a standout performance—catching seven passes for 111 yards. Who was he?

19. What longtime Viking mascot got his job when he simply walked past security guards at Super Bowl IV, with the guards assuming he was the official team mascot?

20. In Super Bowl VIII, it didn't take Miami long to take control. The Dolphins took the opening kickoff and drove 62 yards on 10 plays. Who scored the first touchdown?

21. Following a Viking punt, the Dolphins put together another 10-play drive for a score. Who scored that touchdown?

22. With the Vikings trailing, 17-0, in the second quarter, the team mounted its first drive of the game, but it ended with a fumble on the Miami 6-yard line. Who fumbled the ball and who recovered it?

23. The Dolphins went up, 24-0, in the third quarter when who scored a touchdown?

24. The Vikings scored their only touchdown of the game in the fourth quarter. Who scored it?

25. What two Super Bowl records did Larry Csonka set that day?

26. Who was the Vikings' leading rusher in that game?

27. What were Bob Griese's passing numbers for the game?

28. What Viking led all receivers with five catches in that game?

29. The Vikings and Steelers were locked in a defensive battle in Super Bowl IX until the game's first score came midway through the second quarter. Who scored the game's first points?

30. What two aspects of that play made Super Bowl history?

31. The Steelers took advantage of a Viking turnover on the opening kickoff of the second half. Who fumbled that kickoff and who recovered?

32. The Steelers converted that turnover into a touchdown to take control of the game. Who scored that touchdown?

33. The Vikings only score of that game was the first score in Super Bowl history on a blocked punt. Who blocked the punt, who recovered the punt and who was the punter who had the dubious achievement in the record books?

34. With the Vikings trailing, 9-6, late in the game, the Vikings were convinced they forced Franco Harris to fumble? What player to this day swears he ripped the ball loose before Harris hit the ground?

35. Instead, the Steelers retained possession and put the game away with a touchdown with 3:31 to play. Who scored that touchdown?

36. The Vikings set two records for ineptitude that day. How many total yards did the Viking offense gain and how many of those came rushing?

37. How many of Fran Tarkenton's passes got batted down by Steeler defenders?

38. Franco Harris set two records that day. What were they?

39. How many yards did Chuck Foreman gain in Super Bowl IX?

40. How many of Fran Tarkenton's 27 passes did he complete in Super Bowl IX?

41. In the days leading up to Super Bowl IX, three Vikings made Super Bowl prankster history by dumping garbage cans full of water on the head of ABC telecaster Howard Cosell—retribution for Cosell's constant attention to Fran Tarkenton during Super Bowl week. Who were these three hooligans?

42. How many television viewers were estimated in the record crowd that watched Super Bowl XI?

43. Super Bowl XI was scoreless until the second quarter, when the Raiders scored 16 points. How did they get those points?

44. The Vikings trailed, 19-0, before putting their first points on the board. How did the Vikings finally score in the third quarter?

45. The Raiders scored twice more in the fourth quarter. Who scored the first of those two touchdowns?

46. The second touchdown set a Super Bowl record? What made that play famous?

47. The Vikings finally scored a second touchdown in a Super Bowl in the closing seconds of the game. Who scored that touchdown?

48. The Viking special teams set a famous first in that game. What was it?

49. Erroll Mann set a record in that game that may never be touched.

What was that record?

50. What Raider running back rambled for 137 yards in that game?

51. Who was the M.V.P. of Super Bowl IV?

52. Who was the M.V.P. of Super Bowl VIII?

53. Who was the M.V.P. of Super Bowl IX?

54. Who was the M.V.P. of Super Bowl XI?

55. By the end of the 1976 season, what other team had matched the Vikings' four Super Bowl appearances?

56. Who were the only two head coaches to coach in more Super Bowls than Bud Grant?

57. Only three quarterbacks have had more interceptions in Super Bowls than the six thrown by Fran Tarkenton in his three games. Two of those—John Elway and Jim Kelly—did it in four games. But one did it in only two. Can you name him?

58. What Viking is tied with several other players for a Super Bowl record two career fumble recoveries?

59. The Vikings' six points versus Pittsburgh was the second-lowest point total in Super Bowl history. Who was the only team to score less points?

60. The Vikings set a Super Bowl record for least first downs in a game that was later tied by Miami in its 27-17 loss to Washington in Super Bowl XVII. Against which team did the Vikings have this dubious distinction and how many first downs did they pick up?

61. Against which team or teams did the Vikings set a record by picking up only two rushing first downs?

62. Is the Vikings' 119 total yards against Pittsburgh still a Super Bowl record for least yards gained in a game?

6

THEY'RE BREAKING UP THAT OLD GANG OF MINE

T he loss to the Raiders in Super Bowl XI led to a decline in the Vikings that would last for almost a decade. When linebacker Roy Winston retired following the 1976 season it started a process that would result in a complete changing of the guard in Viking Country over the next three seasons. No less than 10 key players from the Vikings' glory years would be gone by the end of the 1979 season.

The Vikings' decline wasn't immediate because, back in the days before free agency, teams were built and aged together. The Purple People Eaters, the offensive line, the secondary and the quarterbacks were all getting long in the tooth and would result in a systematic plan to begin replacing them.

The plan actually started in 1974, when the Vikings drafted linebackers Matt Blair and Fred McNeill and tackle Steve Riley. In 1975, defensive end Mark Mullaney was brought in as an eventual replacement for Carl Eller or Jim Marshall—whichever broke down first. In 1976, James "Duck" White was hoped to breathe new life into the Purple People Eaters, but history did not view him as much of an addition. Wide receiver Sammy White was the best pick of that season, as the Vikings overhauled their receiving game with the addition of him and Ahmad Rashad. But it was 1977 that the old Purple Gang began realize that change was in the air.

Fran Tarkenton was getting old and the Vikings needed an eventual replacement. For that reason, the team used its top pick of the 1977 college draft on a cocky, self-assured quarterback from Rice University named Tommy Kramer. It was the only time in team history that a No. 1 pick was used to select a quarterback and Kramer would soon become the focal point of the Viking offense. In that same year, the Vikings got a late-round steal when they scooped Scott Studwell on the ninth round in hopes he could make the team and contribute. He ended up being the leading tackler in team history.

But Bud Grant wasn't going to hurry any of his youngsters into the lineup. He had a hard and fast rule about not allowing rookies to start, a practice that had only one major exception—Chuck Foreman.

In 1977, there was no reason to alter the chemistry that had helped the Vikings get to the Super Bowl in three of the previous four seasons. But the decline was becoming obvious. The Vikings fell to 9-5 in 1977, winning the Central Division on a tie-breaker over the Bears, yet had a 1-4 record against teams that made the playoffs that season. The Vikings overcame a five-game stretch at mid-season in which they lost three games to win three of their final four games to make the playoffs—without Tarkenton. Tarkenton suffered the first major injury of his career—a broken leg that opened the door for Kramer.

If anything, Kramer was the epitome of the never-say-die spirit that he embodied on and off the field. His coming out party came against San Francisco on a brutal December afternoon at Met Stadium. With starter Bob Lee struggling and the Vikings trailing, 24-7, early in the fourth quarter, Grant obliged the frostbitten fans' pleas of "We want Tommy" and gave Kramer his shot. He responded with a three-touchdown performance and lifted the Vikings to a 28-27 win over the Niners and helped send the Vikings to the playoffs.

One of the primary differences between 1977 and previous years was that the Vikings would have to go on the road for the playoffs. After making the Rams come to Minnesota for three playoff games during the glory years—winning all three, including two wins to go to Super Bowls— the Vikings had to go to Los Angeles for the first round of the playoffs. After a 35-3 hammering during the regular season, the Vikings weren't given much hope. But, the game turned out to be more like Viking weather than California weather, as a driving rainstorm turned the field into a quagmire of slop and the Vikings dominated. The Purple Gang defense and the Viking rushing attack came up big to lead the Vikes to a 14-7 upset—again kindling the hopes of Viking fans that yet another Super Bowl trip was in the offing.

That dream crashed down with a 23-6 thumping of the Vikings by Dallas and spelled the beginning of the end of Minnesota supremacy. It would be the last time in a decade that the Vikings would be back in an NFC championship game and the dismantling of the team would begin in earnest the next season.

The 1978 season was the official start of the changing of the guard. Kicker Fred Cox retired and guard Ed White moved to San Diego to create a pair of openings in the regular lineup and Tarkenton was back for his final season—knowing an impatient Kramer was waiting in the wings. The Vikings' past was slipping away into memories—a point punctuated when the Vikings brass told Alan Page he didn't have it anymore. Page differed and proved his point—going to the Bears and continuing his glorious career despite slimming down to less than 220 pounds.

The Vikings again won the Central Division, but for a second straight year, they had to back into the title—beating Green Bay on a tie-breaker with 8-7-1 records. The decline of the Vikings was no more obvious than in the final month of the season. The Vikings finished 1-3-1 in their last five games and, after dominating the Rams in the playoffs for a decade, took one on the chin hard—getting pounded, 34-10, to make a quick playoff exit. Other exits would follow.

After releasing Page in the middle of the 1978 season, Carl Eller was sent packing to Seattle following the year. Tarkenton and iron man center Mick Tingelhoff retired and the Vikings began to take on a new look. The dominance was gone, much of the swagger was gone and, to the chagrin of their fans, so were many of the wins.

The retooling of the team continued in 1979. Foreman no longer showed the flashes of brilliance that had made him a star and the Vikings drafted Ted Brown to be his replacement. The team also drafted Notre Dame center David Huffman to replace Tingelhoff, but Huffman would find his niche elsewhere on the line. The team also made another late-round find in tight end Joe Senser. Yet, none of the three would make much of an impact in 1979, as the Vikings fell on hard times for the first time since the 1967 season.

With Kramer learning his craft as a full-time starter, he struggled. The once-mighty Viking defense allowed 21 or more points in 10 of 16 games

—as many as they had in the 84 games from 1969 to 1974. From the start of October until mid-November, the Vikings lost five of six games and were never a factor in the playoff hunt. But the biggest news in 1979 came from off the field. Bowing to pressure that the Vikings would move to Memphis, the Minnesota Legislature approved a domed stadium for the Vikings and Twins. The groundbreaking came in December as the Vikings closed out a dreadful 7-9 season and the days of snow-covered sidelines and flame throwers were going to be over. And along with it was going to go one of the greatest home-field advantages the game has ever known.

The exodus would continue following the 1979 season. Retired were Jim Marshall, Paul Krause and Wally Hilgenberg and Foreman was traded to try to revive his career elsewhere. New faces included defensive linemen Randy Holloway and Doug Martin—a pair of No. 1 draft choices—and cornerbacks John Turner and Willie Teal—a pair of No. 2 draftees. The Vikings front office was committed to winning through defense, but it was going to be on Kramer's back to win enough games to get Minnesota to the post-season.

Kramer sparked a playoff run in 1980—a year with all the earmarks of another disappointment. Heading into November, the Vikings were 3-5 and looked to be going nowhere. But the Viking offense came to life and hopes began to pick up. A three-game winning streak in which the Vikings outscored Washington, Detroit and Tampa Bay, 111-44, moved the Vikings into playoff position at 6-5. Following a loss to Green Bay, road wins at New Orleans and Tampa Bay set the stage for one of the greatest single plays in Vikings history.

The Vikings could clinch a division title with a home win over Cleveland and it was a win the team needed badly. The final game was at Houston, where Earl Campbell was tearing up the league and most observers gave the Vikings little hope to win that game. But, even a win over Cleveland looked bleak. Trailing, 23-22, with 20 seconds to play, the Vikings completed a hook-and-ladder pass from Kramer to Joe Senser to Ted Brown for 34 yards to get the Vikings to the Cleveland 46-yard line with time for one play—a Hail Mary bomb. The Vikings were one of the few teams at the time that routinely practiced such a play called "Squadron Right/Left"—sending three receivers to one side of the field and letting the ball fly. The idea was that the pack would tip the ball and a Viking would make the catch. Rarely are plays drawn up that work so perfectly on the field. As time ran out, Cleveland defensive backs swarmed in the end zone.

That ball was tipped and Ahmad Rashad made a one-handed grab on the 3-yard line and danced in for a touchdown, giving the Vikings a 28-23 win and sending them back to the playoffs.

As was the case in 1978, the Vikings' trip to the playoffs was brief—the Eagles dispatched Minnesota 31-16 and Vikings' fans came to the realization that, if Minnesota was ever going to get back to the Super Bowl, it would have to be through the building process that got them there a decade before and the current cast wasn't going to do it.

The 1981 season was as close to a Jekyll-Hyde season as the Vikings have ever had—one week they looked so good and the next they looked hideous. The year started with losses to Tampa Bay and Oakland, but then Kramer led the Vikings to five straight wins—including a two-point win over Detroit, a three-point victory over Chicago and a two-point triumph over San Diego. Following consecutive losses and consecutive wins, the Vikings stood at 7-4 with five to play—only one of these teams sporting with a winning record.

The result? The Vikings lost all five games, many of which came in the same fashion in which they had won games earlier in the season—a 31-30 loss at Atlanta, a 10-9 loss at Chicago and a 10-6 loss against Kansas City in the season finale. The disappointment was evident on all the fans' faces following the loss to Kansas City—a nationally-televised Saturday afternoon game in which it was later learned Kramer had been out partying until the early morning hours. Vikings fans were still unaccustomed to losing. While the Vikings had not been overpowering for four years, five-game losing streaks didn't happen in Minnesota—which was one reason fans were saddened. But it was the second reason that will stick with many of the old dyed-in-the-wool purple faithful.

That loss would mark the final game at the old Met. It was going to be officially abandoned for the new Metrodome in downtown Minneapolis. The days of snowmobile suits, Sorel boots, parkas, double-lined choppers, stocking caps, wool scarves and flasks of adult beverages to warm up the frozen fans, and hours of pre-game and post-game tailgating were over. If the last three seasons weren't a painful enough reminder that the Vikings weren't the power team that had run roughshod over the league for the better part of three presidencies, the Reagan era of the 1980s was to bring about change. Chief among them to Viking fans was the loss of the unprecedented Met Stadium advantage in November, December and January.

Fans stayed around after the game longer than usual. Some milled around on the field, since security guards figured there was nothing to protect since the stadium was coming down anyway. Others came equipped with tools and left the Met with their favorite seat. Others just sat around in the parking lot and talked about the good times they had at the hideous old stadium. Some laughed. Some cried. But they all new it was going to be a new ball game at the Metrodome—and they were right. Outdoor football as the players and fans had known it was dead.

TRIVIA QUESTIONS

1. What distinction did the Vikings and Los Angeles Rams have in 1977 that has happened with only two other teams in Viking history—St. Louis is 1972 and Washington in 1992?

2. On October 24, 1977, the Vikings got blown out, 35-3, in a game against the Rams at Los Angeles. When was the last time prior to that game that the Vikings had lost a game by more than 32 points?

3. This player led the Vikings in tackles in 1977—the only year he would lead the team in that category?

4. In 1977, Fran Tarkenton missed the final five games of the season with the first serious injury of his career. As a result, he threw a career-low number of touchdowns. How many TDs did Tark have that year?

5. In 1976, the Vikings played their first overtime game—a game that finished tied, 10-10, with the Rams. In 1977, the team won its first overtime game and lost its first. What team did the Vikings beat to get their first OT win and who did they lose to for their first OT loss?

6. In Tommy Kramer's coming out party against San Francisco, what was the score when he entered the game in the fourth quarter?

7. What was ironic about the timing of the decision to bring Kramer in the game?

8. Kramer threw three touchdowns in the game, including the last two to the same player. Who was the Viking receiver who caught the last two?

9. When the Vikings went to the playoffs in 1977, who was the starting quarterback?

10. In the 14-7 upset of the Rams in the divisional playoff, two Vikings scored rushing touchdowns in the game. Who were they?

11. In that same game, a running back ran for more than 100 yards. Who was he?

12. A week later, the Vikings played Dallas in the NFC Championship game—losing, 23-6. Who accounted for the Vikings' points?

13. The Cowboys had three different players score touchdowns in that game—one you would expect and two lesser-known players. Can you name all three?

14. What was historic about that loss in the NFC title game?

15. The Vikings opened the 1978 season with a 31-24 loss at New Orleans, breaking a 10-year streak since the Saints had last beaten the Vikings. How many games had gone by between New Orleans victories?

16. Two weeks later, the Vikings lost again. What team beat them and what was significant about that home loss?

17. Less than a month after that, the Vikings picked up a dubious distinction in a 29-28 loss. What team rallied late to win the game and what made the loss a memory Viking fans would like to forget?

18. On October 22, 1978, the Vikings beat Green Bay, 21-7. What was significant about that victory?

19. In 1978, the Vikings were outscored by their opponents 306-294. When was the last time prior to that season that the Vikes had been outscored by the opposition?

20. When was the last time prior to the Vikings doing it in 1978 that a team had won its division while being outscored by its opponents?

21. The Vikings went into Los Angeles with the worst division champion winning percentage in league history, and they got hammered, 34-10. What was the score at halftime?

22. Who accounted for the Vikings' points in that game?

23. Prior to that loss, what was the Vikings' playoff record against the Rams?

24. Four different Rams scored touchdowns in that game and people could bet good money that even the hardest of hardcore Rams fans couldn't name them all. How many can you get?

25. The game's M.V.P. was a defensive back who made two interceptions of Fran Tarkenton passes deep in Rams' territory to snuff out Viking drives. Who was this player?

26. Tarkenton's playing career ended that day. On his final drive with less than two minutes to play, what did Tarkenton do?

27. Tarkenton's final season was not a memorable one. He set a career high for interceptions that season. How passes did he have picked off that year?

28. Tarkenton and the pass-happy Viking attack set several team records that year and Francis was near the top in several categories for NFL quarterbacks. In which did he lead the NFL?

29. 1978 was also Foreman's last with the Vikings—a season in which he ran for a career-low in yardage. How many yards did Foreman rush for in 1978?

30. In 1978, a Viking set a reception record that stood for 16 years. Who was this Viking and how many catches did he have in 1978?

31. The Vikings' special teams underwent drastic change in 1978, as the team brought in a new kicker, punter and return specialist. Can you name all three?

32. 1978 was also the last time Bobby Bryant would lead the team in interceptions when he picked off seven. How many seasons did Bryant lead the Vikings in interceptions in his career?

33. How many times did Paul Krause lead the Vikings in interceptions?

34. 1978 also marked the first season in team history that one of the Purple People Eaters didn't lead the team in sacks. Who was that player?

35. Prior to his leading the team in sacks, the title had always gone to either Jim Marshall, Alan Page or Carl Eller. You'll need four answers for this one—How many times did Page lead the team in sacks? Eller? Marshall? Finally, in 1963, Marshall tied for the team lead with what player?

36. Late in the 1978 regular season, the Vikings allowed Detroit 45 points in a 45-14 drubbing. When was the last time the Vikings had allowed more than 45 points in a game?

37. During his career with the Vikings, how many 100-yard rushing games did Chuck Foreman have?

38. How many 100-yard receiving games did Foreman have?

39. What was the Vikings record in games where Foreman ran or received for 100 yards?

40. How many 300-yard passing games did Tarkenton have in his career with the Vikings?

41. What was the team's record in games in which he threw for 300 or more yards?

42. During the Vikings' glory years, they wrapped division titles

primarily because they beat up the Central Division. In 1979, when the Vikings finished 7-9, what was their record against division opponents?

43. 1979 was only the second time in 12 seasons that the Vikings had not won the NFC Central title. Who won it the two years the Vikings didn't in that span?

44. What player led the Vikings in tackles in 1979? Hint: It was the only year he ever did.

45. Before the player above led the team in tackles, a player at his position had not done so since 1965. Who was that player?

46. How many touchdowns did Tommy Kramer throw in his first year as a full-time starter?

47. In 1979, this player became the first player other than Chuck Forman to lead the team in rushing since Foreman's arrival. Who was this back?

48. In 1980, following two weeks in which the Vikings totaled only three points, the team went on a tear—scoring 39, 34 and 38 points in consecutive games. When was the last time the Vikings scored 34 or more points in three consecutive games?

49. In the home finale in 1980, Kramer carved out his own niche in Viking lore with his Hail Mary pass to Ahmad Rashad. What three Viking receivers were lined up in the fabled "Squadron Right"?

50. The play didn't go as planned, since two receivers were held up at the line of scrimmage. Before the ball got to Rashad, only one player touched it. Who was it?

51. Rashad was famous for yelling something repeatedly after the catch. What was he yelling and what was the significance of the remark?

52. Tommy Kramer set two records that day—one that still stands. What were those records?

53. The Vikings went to Philadelphia and were defeated, 31-16, by the Eagles. What was the halftime score?

54. Who scored the Vikings' points in that game?

55. How many fumbles did the Vikings have in the regular season in 1980?

56. How many did they have in the second half against the Eagles?

57. The Vikings set a modern playoff record for most turnovers in one half, much less the 22 minutes it took them to achieve this unwanted record. How many turnovers did the Vikings have in the final 22 minutes of that game?

58. In 1980, this Viking kick returner set Viking records for most kickoff returns and most yards gained. Do you know him?

59. In 1980, this player led the team in tackles for the first time. A year later he would set a team record for most total tackles. Can you name him?

60. The Vikings opened the 1981 season with consecutive losses. When was the last time the Vikes had started a season 0-2?

61. That same season, the Vikings went on a five-game winning streak. When was the last time the team had a longer winning streak?

62. The Vikings ended the 1981 season with a five-game losing streak. When was the last time the Vikings had lost five consecutive games in a season?

63. In the final three games of 1981, the Vikings scored a total of 22 points, being held to nine, seven and six points, respectively. When was the last time the Vikings had been held under 10 points in three straight games?

64. In 1981, he became the only Viking other than Chuck Foreman to

run for 1,000 yards in a season. Name him?

65. This player moved into the No. 2 position all-time on the Vikings single-season receptions list when he caught 83 passes in 1981. Who was he?

66. In 1981, the Vikings moved to a new practice facility built especially for them. What is the name of this facility and where is it located?

67. Who scored the last Viking touchdown at Met Stadium?

68. Who scored the last points at Met Stadium?

69. What is on the site today that the old Met Stadium once sat?

7

THERE'S NO PLACE LIKE DOME

I t seemed unheard of at the time and it was something that made longtime players like Bill Brown and Jim Marshall look up with disgust—a Teflon roof over the Vikings' stadium. But as the 1982 season began, that's where the Vikings found themselves. It was a home that marked change and served as a metaphor for the entire state of the NFL. As one famous Minnesotan said years earlier, "The times, they are a-changin'."

Over the next seven seasons, the Vikings would say goodbye to Bud Grant—twice—endure a pair of player strikes, survive the threat of a rival league, suffer through turmoil at the top levels of management and make a trade that would forever change the fortunes of two franchises—forcing the Vikings to go years without top draft picks and help make the Dallas Cowboys the closest thing to a dynasty the NFL had seen since the Steelers of the 1970s.

The 1982 season was a particularly bittersweet season for the NFL, including the Vikings. It seemed for a while that the entire season would be lost, as the players and owners met an impasse two weeks into the season and the players went out on strike for more than two months. When it was finally settled, the league had to scramble to save the season. The result? A wide open, 16-team playoff tournament that would allow every team with a winning record and two with losing records—Detroit and Cleveland— into the playoff party—or parity depending on your point of view.

Because of scheduling quirks that worked out, the Vikings played only five of their nine games that season against NFC teams so, despite losing three of four games to the AFC, and being able to string consecutive wins together only once, the Vikings not only made the playoffs, they hosted a first-round game against Atlanta. The Vikings won that game, but all that earned them was a date with eventual Super Bowl champion Washington. The Skins pounded the Vikings, 21-7, and never looked back. That season took a toll on Bud Grant and led to a momentous decision.

Late in the 1983 season, Grant, whose Vikings had started 6-2 only to lose six of the next seven games, lost the zest for coaching. He called all of his assistants together for a dinner and told them he was through. He said he would go to bat for all of them to be retained, but that he had seen enough. The game was not the same fun it had been and he was ready to call it quits. The Vikings' 8-8 finish that year was especially painful. After years on the top rung of the NFC ladder, Grant's Vikings had gone 44-42-1 over the previous six seasons and Grant was tired of mediocrity. That, combined with growing tension on the Vikings' Board of Directors that hamstrung his friend Max Winter, hastened Grant's exit from the game.

The front office was undergoing some divisive changes. Over three years, original ownership members Bill Boyer and H.P. Skoglund died and Bernie Ritter removed himself from active status. With Winter's faculties diminishing, the designated replacements for Boyer, Skoglund and Ritter voted Mike Lynn into operational control of the team, essentially leaving Winter on the outside looking in at the team he had built.

About the only thing worse than the management strife at the time was the product put forth on the field. The 1984 season was the worst in the history of the Vikings and one of the worst ever by a non-expansion team. Grant had asked that longtime confidante and offensive coordinator Jerry Burns be given the head coaching job, but that instead went to receivers coach Les Steckel—a former Marine who treated his players as if they were recruits. Game days became picnics compared to the horrors the players endured on the practice field. Steckel devised an obstacle course designed to test the mettle of his players. Instead, it broke them.

It was obvious early on in 1984 that the Vikings were in trouble. They lost their final three pre-season games by a combined score of 91-17. After starting the regular season 2-2, the bottom dropped out. The Vikings lost five straight games and, following a come-from-behind 27-24 win over lowly Tampa Bay, the Vikings lost their last five games by scores of 45-17,

42-21, 34-3, 31-17, 51-7, and 38-14. The humiliation was too much for the players and fans to bear. Steckel was hastily sent packing and the plea went out for Grant to return—both for player morale and to keep the fan base that was quickly bailing out on the Vikings. It took some arm-twisting, but Grant relented and returned for the 1985 season.

Grant's comeback was bolstered by Lynn's bold moves in the market to scoop players from the failed USFL. Lynn made all the right moves, picking up future Viking stars in Anthony Carter, former Viking draft pick Keith Millard and Gary Zimmerman off the USFL roster of stars and adding rookies Chris Doleman, Issiac Holt and Kirk Lowdermilk in the 1985 draft. The Vikings began the rebuilding process with a bang.

The Vikings didn't set the world on fire in 1985—finishing 7-9—but they returned to respectability and set the foundation for future success. Having done the job he was asked to do, Grant again settled back into retirement to his deer stand and duck blind and, this time, Jerry Burns got the head coaching job.

"Burnsie," as he was affectionately referred to by players, was a departure from Grant. A crusty Burgess Meredith look-alike, Burns could buddy up to you in a second and, if someone questioned him or his players, he defended them vigorously—often with a string of obscenities that could make a longshoreman blush in horror. In his first season, the Vikings began to turn the corner. Tommy Kramer had one of his finest years as a pro, Joey Browner, Millard, Doleman and Scott Studwell were becoming dominating defensive powers and the result was evident on the field. The Vikings started by winning three of their first four games and won three of their final four to finish 9-7—outscoring their opponents by a whopping 125 points (398-273). At the end of that season, it was believed that the Vikings were only a step away from being one of the power teams of the league. The Bears were still the class of the division, but the gap was closing. Then came 1987—a season the Vikings never prepared for.

From the opening days of training camp, the word was out that another player strike was imminent. It was widely reported in the media and was a constant topic of discussion with players, coaches and owners. As the drop-dead date approached, it became apparent to everyone that, barring an 11th-hour miracle, there was going to be another strike. Everyone, that is, except Lynn. He was convinced there would be a resolution before a strike, considering the public black eye the league took due to the 1982 work stoppage. It would turn out to be the second-worst decision of his career.

The Vikings started the season 2-0 and the team was confident that this would be the year the Vikings would topple the Bears as divisional king of the hill. But then the strike hit and the Vikings were unprepared. While other teams had made arrangements for replacement players, the Vikings were caught without contingency plans waiting in the wings. Lynn hastily prepared workouts in Memphis, which turned out to be a cattle call reminiscent of the Norm Van Brocklin inaugural training camp in Bemidji. No team in the NFL had a bigger collection of dregs than the Vikings. The situation got worse as word came down from the league office that the replacement games would count in the standings. The Vikings went 0-3, being outscored, 70-33, and what had started out so promising had turned sour quickly.

When the players came back, the Vikings won five of six games. Instead of being 7-1, they were 7-4 and hopelessly behind the Bears. They would have to go through the playoffs on the road as a wild card and were given no shot at winning. As it turned out, that was the break they needed.

In the first round of the playoffs, nobody knew who would start at quarterback—the injured Tommy Kramer or his understudy Wade Wilson. The mystery served the Vikings well, as the team dissected New Orleans, 44-10. Then they went to San Francisco and shocked the top-seeded 49ers, 36-24, to advance to the NFC title game. Fans fresh off a Twins World Series win were back on the bandwagon. But, the Vikings would lose to the Redskins, 17-10, as their Super Bowl hopes slipped away on a dropped pass at the goal line by Darrin Nelson in the final minutes of the game. Although disappointed, the Vikings were on the brink of being a Super Bowl team again and the old days of purple and gold were back.

That dream would continue to bloom in 1988. While the Bears again won the division with a 12-4 record, two of those four losses came to the Vikings—including a 31-7 hammering at Soldier Field. During one four-game stretch late in the season, the powerful Vikings outscored their opponents, 123-9, and looked almost unbeatable. But following a playoff win over the Rams, the Vikings again traveled to Candlestick Park, where the Wade Wilson-led Vikings got beat up, 34-9, by the 49ers and again spent an off-season wondering what it would take to get to the Super Bowl.

Following a slow 2-2 start in 1989, Lynn had an idea. He looked at his defense and saw one of the best units in the league. He saw a rock solid offensive line. He saw a quarterback unit of Kramer, Wilson and Rich Gannon that was deep, effective and versatile. He saw an impressive receiver corps of Anthony Carter, Hassan Jones and tight end Steve Jordan. One thing was missing—a featured running back that could carry the mail 25 times a game. Lynn had an idea and was hell-bent to get it done.

So, on October 12, 1989, Lynn and the Dallas Cowboys consummated the biggest blockbuster trade the league had ever seen. Not since Ollie Mattson had been traded for a dozen players had such a deal gone down. The Vikings traded five players, first- and second-round draft picks in 1990, 1991, and 1992 and a third-rounder in 1992 to get Herschel Walker and four late-round picks. The Vikings had nine Pro Bowlers from the previous year and Walker was viewed as the one player the team needed. On the day of the trade, a grinning Lynn told the stunned media assembled at the press conference that couldn't believe the terms of the trade, "This trade will be judged one way. If we win the Super Bowl, it was a good trade. If we don't, it wasn't."

What Lynn failed to realize was that, at the time, the Bears were still a couple of years from declining and the 49ers were going to be one of the all-time great teams. For all his bravado and tough talk, Lynn's Vikings would never be more than a wild card until the Bears came down and a playoff casualty until the 49ers weakened. Neither would happen as quickly as he hoped.

After a strong start, the Vikings and Walker settled into a comfortable 10-6 record—good enough for second place in the NFC Central and yet another trip to San Francisco, where they got crushed, 41-13, by the Niners. That loss seemed to shatter what the Vikings had built up. In 1990, the Vikings had a five-game losing streak early in the season to start 1-6 and, despite a strong finish, ended up 6-10. A similar fate awaited them in 1991, as the Vikings lost three straight games early to come out of the gate 2-4. Fingers began being pointed. This guy wasn't doing his job. That guy wasn't doing his. Leadership was nowhere to be found. The Vikings were in disarray and change was needed.

Burns was the first to go, stepping down after being so close and ending up so far away. Several of the complacent, talented individuals would follow. Without any blue chip talent coming in, the Vikings seemed destined to be in a rut for years to come. They needed a change. That came in the form of a fiery coach with a drum set and a motivational approach to the game not seen in Viking country since Van Brocklin's early days. His name was Denny Green and, as he said in his first interview upon being hired, "There's a new sheriff in town."

TRIVIA QUESTIONS

1. After what political figure was the Metrodome named after?

2. On what date was the first Vikings game played at the Metrodome?

3. Who was the opponent in that pre-season game and what was the final score?

4. Who scored the first touchdown in the Metrodome?

5. The Vikings regular-season opener was the first "official" game in the Metrodome on September 12, 1982. Who was the opponent and what was the final score?

6. Who scored the first regular-season touchdown in the Metrodome?

7. How many divisional games did the Vikings play in 1982 and what was their record in those games?

8. What was the Vikings home record in 1982?

9. In the first round of the strike-designed playoff format, the Vikings hosted Atlanta. What seed were the Vikings?

10. What was the final score of that game?

11. What was unusual about the Falcons' scoring in that game?

12. How many times did the lead change hands in that game?

13. Tommy Kramer threw for 253 yards in that game and tossed a pair of touchdowns. Who caught them?

14. The Vikings trailed, 24-23, until they drove 72 yards in the closing minutes. Who scored the eventual game-winning touchdown with 1:44 to play?

15. The Vikings got steam rolled against Washington in the second round of the playoffs. What was the final score?

16. Who was the game's unquestioned M.V.P. and why was it so obvious that he be selected?

17. Who scored the Vikings only points in that game?

18. What Viking rookie led the team in kickoff returns in 1982?

19. On September 8, 1983, the Vikings lost, 48-17, to San Francisco. How long had it been since the Vikings had allowed that many points?

20. In a span of six games in 1983, the Vikings had road wins at Tampa Bay and at Green Bay. What made those wins noteworthy?

21. On December 5, 1983, the Vikings lost to the Detroit Lions. What about the score made it so unique that it had never happened before or since?

22. In 1983—his only year with the Vikings—this kicker led the team with 108 points. Who was he?

23. This player led the Vikings with 51 receptions in 1983—the only year he would ever lead the team in that category. Can you name him?

24. In 1983, this quarterback led the Vikings for the only year in his career, replacing an injured Tommy Kramer. Who was he?

25. The Vikings won only three games in 1984. What teams did they beat?

26. Incredibly, the Vikings' 3-13 record was the third-worst in the NFL in 1984. What two teams were even more pathetic, sporting 2-14 records?

27. How many times did the Vikings give up 30 or more points in 1984?

28. How many times did the Vikings score 17 or less points in 1984?

29. In 1984, this running back became the first rookie other than Chuck Foreman to lead the team in rushing. Who was he?

30. This Viking led the team in receiving in 1984, the only time in his 11-year career that he would lead the team. Name him.

31. These two players tied for the team lead in sacks in 1984 with six apiece. Who were they?

32. In Bud Grant's regular-season return in 1985 as head coach, the Vikings won, 28-21. Who was the opponent and what made the victory an achievement for the Vikes?

33. On November 11, 1985, the Packers beat the Vikings, 27-17. What made that loss one that sent archivists back a long way?

34. On December 1, 1985, the Vikings defeated Philadelphia, 28-23. What made this victory one for the record books?

35. What Viking led the team in scoring in 1985—the second straight year he had the team's most points?

36. In 1985, this rookie led the team in kickoff returns for the only time in his career. Who was he?

37. In 1986, Jerry Burns was hired as head coach. He had been an offensive coordinator under Grant since he came to Minnesota. Under whom did he coach prior to coming to Minnesota?

38. During Burns' tenure as head coach, he maintained the same offensive and defensive coordinators. Who were they?

39. On November 2, 1986, Tommy Kramer put his name in the record books for being the first player in NFL history to accomplish a passing feat. What did he do in that 44-38 overtime loss to the Redskins?

40. By far the smallest attendance of any Vikings home game came during the replacement game during the strike year of 1987. Who was the opponent and what was the approximate attendance at that game? (You can't be expected to know the exact number.)

41. Who was the replacement quarterback when the real Vikings were on strike?

42. After seeing how horrible the replacement team was, who did Mike Lynn unsuccessfully try to get Jerry Burns to name quarterback?

43. His lack of foresight to the players strike aside, Lynn had worked his way into the good graces of the Vikings' management. What was Lynn's salary in 1987?

44. Following the end of the players strike, the Vikings played their first game on a Monday night—the first time two Monday Night Football games were played simultaneously. Who did the Vikings play and why did they play on Monday night?

45. What was the Vikings' non-strike record in 1987?

46. In the wild card playoffs in 1987, the Vikings had to play New Orleans. What was the Saints' record in 1987?

47. The Vikings fell behind early, 7-0, but took control of the game thanks to a special teams play. What happened on that play that put the Vikings in the post-season record books?

48. The Vikings blew the game open in the second quarter by scoring three touchdowns. Who scored them?

49. The Vikings kicker helped salt the game away with field goals of 42, 32, and 19 yards. Who was that kicker?

50. This running back scored the game's final touchdown on an 8-yard run to give the Vikes a 44-10 win. Who was he?

51. The Vikings set a post-season team record for time of possession in that game. Of the 60 minutes, how long did the Vikings have the ball?

52. The Vikings also forced Bobby Hebert and the Saints offense to cough up the ball too many times. How many turnovers did the Viking defense create in that game?

53. In the divisional playoffs the next week, the Vikings faced the heavily-favored 49ers. What was San Francisco's record in 1987?

54. The Vikings again took control of the game in the second quarter after being tied 3-3 after one quarter. The Vikings scored 17 points in the second quarter. How did they score them?

55. The 49ers never got within 10 points the rest of the way. The Vikings added 16 second-half points to win, 36-24. How did they score those points?

56. For a second straight week, Anthony Carter put himself in the post-season record books. What did he do to set a post-season record?

57. In the NFC championship game in 1987, the Vikings never led. Who scored Washington's first touchdown?

58. The game was tied, 7-7, at halftime after the Vikings came back with a touchdown of their own. How did they score?

59. Following an exchange of field goals, the Redskins scored the game-winning touchdown with five minutes to play. Who scored that touchdown?

60. The Vikings drove to the Washington 6-yard line in the final minute before Nelson dropped the fourth-down pass on the 1-yard line. Who was defending Nelson on that play and slapped away the ball when it came off Nelson's hands?

61. The Redskins defense spent much of the day in Wade Wilson's face. How many times was Wilson sacked in that game?

62. In 1988, the Viking front office came under fire when four new members joined the board—two who would stay on and two who would eventually leave. Who were those four men?

63. In 1988, the Vikings were about as predictably oppressive as any team in the league, blowing out all of their lesser opponents. How many teams did the Vikings beat by 23 or more points in 1988?

64. How many NFC teams had a better record in 1988 than the Vikings?

65. The Vikings played the Rams in the first round of the playoffs in 1988 and this player made two first-quarter interceptions that led to a pair of Viking touchdowns. Who was he?

66. The Vikings converted those interceptions into touchdowns scored by whom?

67. The Vikings put the 28-17 win out of reach with a pair of second-half touchdowns. Who scored them?

68. The Vikings got drilled, 34-9, the next week against the 49ers. San Francisco built a 21-3 halftime lead, scoring three first-half touchdowns. Who scored them?

69. The Vikings got their only touchdown of the game in the third quarter. Who scored it?

70. The 49ers added two more touchdowns in the fourth quarter. Who scored them?

71. In 1988, this Viking intercepted eight passes to lead the team—the only year he would do so. Who was he?

72. This rookie led the Vikings in kick returns in 1988. Who was he?

73. In 1988, this punter became the first punter other than Greg Coleman to kick for the Vikings in 11 seasons. Who was he?

74. This player became only the third Viking to surpass 1,000 yards receiving in a season and set a team record for yards in 1988. Who was he and how many yards did he gain?

75. In 1988, the Vikings leading rusher gained only 380 yards. Who was it?

76. Because of that lack of production, the Vikings made the trade to get Herschel Walker. What Viking players were sent away as part of that trade?

77. The Vikings wound up shelling out their first-round picks in 1990, 1991 and 1992 to get Walker. Who did those picks end up being?

78. The Vikings also received a pair of picks from Dallas. Who did they use to take third-rounders in 1990 and 1991?

79. From October 1 to the end of the 1989 regular season, the Vikings went 9-4. What was unusual about two of those losses?

80. On November 5, 1989, the Vikings set an NFL first that hasn't been duplicated when they defeated the Los Angeles Rams. What happened that day?

81. The Vikings won the division in 1989. How many seasons had it been since Minnesota was on top of the NFC Central?

82 In that span, how many times did the other Central Division teams win the title?

83. The Vikings again advanced to play the 49ers, but this time it was a different story. Joe Montana threw four first-half touchdowns to build a 27-3 halftime lead. Who caught those four TD passes?

84. The Vikings scored only one touchdown in the 41-13 loss. Who scored that TD?

85. In 1990, two of the Vikings owners attempted a hostile takeover of

the team by buying out Max Winter's stock? Who were they?

86. How much did they buy Winter's stock for?

87. These two mavericks would be thwarted in their attempt to take over the ownership because of a fine print clause in the Vikings organizational charter—set up by Mike Lynn. What did Lynn do to keep them effectively out of power?

88. The two eventually settled their court cases with the Vikings and sold their stock back to the ownership group. How much did they sell their stock for less than two years after buying it?

89. The pair that tried the hostile takeover had intended to fire Lynn as team president. Who were they prepared to put into the post had they succeeded?

90. In the 1990 season, the Vikings had successive streaks of winning and losing on their way to a 6-10 season. What were the lengths of those streaks?

91. In the third week of the 1990 season, the Vikings were in what turned out to be the fortunate position of being the first team available to make a pickup off the NFL waiver wire. What player was cut that week that was scooped up by the Vikings?

92. What team had cut him and how much did the Vikings spend to get his rights?

93. In 1991, the Vikings finished 8-8, earning half of those wins by taking two games from a pair of teams. Who were those teams?

94. Lynn left the Vikings following the 1991 season, but he wasn't done working with the NFL. What job did he take when he left the organization?

95. Upon leaving, Lynn suggested the Vikings hire his neighbor as team president. They did. Who was this fortunate man next door?

96. He didn't have a football background, but he had served as a top executive for what two large corporations before coming to the Vikings?

97. What was his first decision as team president?

98. Who was considered the front-runner for the vacant coaching job—to the point that both major Twin Cities newspapers had columnists announce him as becoming the new head coach?

8

GREEN ACRES

W hen the Vikings brought in Dennis Green to be their head coach, many were skeptical. Green had the credentials. He was an assistant under Bill Walsh with the 49ers, had the prized Super Bowl ring that had eluded every coach and player to wear the purple and gold and had successfully taken the dismal Northwestern football program and transformed it into a legitimate contender—not on the level of Ohio State or Michigan, but they weren't the dregs that everybody used to want for the homecoming game.

The reason for the skepticism was that Green came off as being a "rah-rah" type and the Vikings weren't a "rah-rah" team—at least not the team Green inherited. They had a lot of players who made an impact in the locker room, but there wasn't the one player that stood up and said, "I'm the man and you'll listen when I talk." There wasn't a Carl Eller breaking blackboards. There wasn't a Fran Tarkenton calling his own plays. There wasn't a Bill Brown working the players into a froth on the sidelines. There wasn't leadership. Green said he would create it, even if it meant getting rid of the players he viewed as malcontents who enjoyed having Jerry Burns as their best friend.

No truer words were ever spoken. Green didn't care if his players were his friends. Respect to him meant more than friendship and if he had to rock the boat to prove it, he was going to. As history would attest, he did.

Without the benefit of any top draft picks as a residual backlash of the

Herschel Walker trade, Green cleaned house. His first team had 17 new players on it and some of the discontented veterans were sent packing— including Walker, Wade Wilson, and Joey Browner.

The conventional wisdom was that the Vikings were going to stink up the joint. Green had overhauled the team on the fly and it was almost unanimously believed that the Vikings were going to need two or three years to recover. The problem was nobody remembered to tell Green or the Vikings that they were supposed to be horrible. The team started out by winning all four of its pre-season games by combined scores of 140-6 and went on to win five of its first six regular season games in 1992. The Vikings destroyed the division, winning seven of eight games, and when Minnesota beat Pittsburgh in a defensive classic, 6-3, at Three Rivers Stadium, Minnesota was the division champion for only the second time since 1979.

What followed would be the one primary criticism of Green. The Vikings lost in the playoffs, falling, 24-7, to Washington—the second home loss to the Redskins that season. Despite a solid season and a division championship, Minnesota was still a step away from joining the likes of San Francisco, Washington and Dallas at the upper echelon of the NFC. So the changes continued.

Green continued to purge the organization, as disenchanted veterans gave way to Green's hand-picked replacements. Gone were Rich Gannon, Hassan Jones, Kirk Lowdermilk, Mike Merriweather, Darrin Nelson, Al Noga, and Gary Zimmerman. In were running back Robert Smith, wide receiver Qadry Ismail, and guard John Gerak—all rookies. One of Green's main frustrations in 1992 was that all the top teams had a decisive leader at quarterback. The Vikings didn't. Gannon and Sean Salisbury took turns and neither had the starting job wrapped up. So Green went after a veteran who had owned the division for years—ex-Bear Jim McMahon.

With McMahon, the Vikings had a swagger, but it was defense that was the hallmark of the Vikings in 1993. The Vikings continued to pummel the NFC Central—going 6-2—but the magic faded outside the division, as the Vikings lost five of eight games outside the division. But, with the team at 6-7 with three weeks to play, the Vikings again rallied around Green— beating Green Bay on the road, hammering Joe Montana and the Kansas City Chiefs, 30-10, and avenging their playoff loss from the previous year by defeating the Redskins on the road on New Year's Eve to make it back to the playoffs.

But as had happened the previous year, the Vikings fell flat in the playoffs. This time having to go to the New Jersey Meadowlands to play the Giants in near-hurricane conditions, McMahon's battered body crumbled. Knocked out of the game twice with concussions, he came back twice to replace an ineffective Salisbury—only to continue to get assaulted by the G-Men. The Vikings lost, 17-10, and the fans and media started questioning if Green had what it took to win big playoff games. The comparisons to Bud Grant began. Bud, it was theorized, won playoff games even when his teams may not have been as impressive as the opponents. Green didn't have that luxury.

The question of McMahon's long-term durability came into question as the 1994 season approached. Green knew he was right in that the Vikings needed a veteran quarterback and he tapped into another one—making a trade with the Houston Oilers shortly before draft day to get Warren Moon—a savvy veteran who was searching for a Super Bowl ring just like the Vikings. The result was undeniable.

Moon and the Vikings lit up the scoreboard in 1994, as Moon shattered every major Viking passing record that had existed to date and Cris Carter and Jake Reed became the first Viking teammates to catch for 1,000 yards in the same season. The Vikings came out of the gate fast, winning seven of their first nine games and giving fans the impression that this could finally be the team to get the Vikings back to the Super Bowl. Then the roof caved in, as the Vikings lost their next three games and fell hopelessly behind the Cowboys and 49ers for home field advantage. Minnesota rallied to win three its final four games, clinching the Central Division title on the final night of the season against a 49er team resting its starters—putting Minnesota in the playoffs for the third straight year.

The hopes of the third time being the charm were not to be. With Moon hobbled by injuries, the Chicago Bears came into the Metrodome and thumped the Vikings, 35-18, a humiliating loss to a team Green had defeated six straight times. With three straight playoff losses—two at home —the Green dissenters began to come out of the woodwork. That would only increase the following season.

In a move that will be remembered by many Viking fans, the organization released running back Terry Allen—fearing his two surgically-repaired knees did not warrant his $1.5 million contract. Hindsight showed the Vikings were mistaken in that belief, but it allowed Green's first No. 1 draft pick, Robert Smith, to take over the feature-back reigns—at least for those games in which he was healthy.

The 1995 Vikings were a departure from Green's first three teams. After being the strongest team within the division, the Vikings were unable to maintain that control. In their previous playoff years, the Vikings had controlled all playoff tie-breakers by winning their divisional games. In 1995, the opposite was true. After dropping the season opener at Chicago, the Vikings won three of their next four games. The team was 3-2 with three straight divisional games coming up and again hopes were high that the Green magic would come through for the Vikings. Instead, Minnesota lost their next three games and never recovered. Despite winning five of six games following the three-game skid, Minnesota needed to keep winning to make the playoffs. A road loss to San Francisco dropped the Vikings to 8-7 and, with the team leading, 24-3, at Cincinnati at halftime of the season finale, news came to the Vikings that their playoffs hopes had died with a victory by Atlanta. For the first time in Green's tenure, his team actually admitted giving up and were outscored, 24-0, in the second half—one of the lowest moments in his coaching tenure.

Even though the Vikings posted some eye-popping offensive numbers, they were clearly not in the class of the league's top teams and a Central Division rival—the Green Bay Packers—had moved within a breath of being one of those elite teams. It would take one more year out of Moon to keep Minnesota close to the top, especially since the defense was going to undergo radical change with the departure of defensive co-ordinator Tony Dungy to Tampa Bay.

That hope was dashed early when Moon, who had set a goal of an injury-free season, went down with a high ankle sprain in the season opener. The Vikings turned to career backup Brad Johnson, a player who had been denied a starting opportunity behind Rich Gannon, Sean Salisbury, McMahon and Moon in the past. With three of those four gone, the Vikings had little choice but to throw Johnson into the fray and he responded in the 1996 season. He helped the Vikings start the season 4-0, and after Moon returned and was ineffective due to recurring injuries, Johnson rallied Minnesota late to win four of five games to earn a wild-card berth.

For the fourth time in five years, Minnesota was in the playoffs—against a fourth different team in the Dallas Cowboys. The Cowboys showed little mercy on the Vikings, hammering Minnesota, 40-15, and starting serious talk of Green being fired.

After five years of silence about his critics, Green said that was going to change in 1997. Unwilling to accept the continued criticism of his coaching, Green came out with a scathing book—one that ripped the Vikings ownership group, claimed the media was orchestrated in having him removed as head coach and even providing a plan to sue the team for ownership. It engulfed his team in controversy, but you couldn't tell it on the field.

With Johnson re-signed long-term and Moon shown the door, Minnesota strung together a six-game winning streak to move to 8-2. But then the Vikings fell as flat as they had in years, dropping five games in a row, including a two-point loss to the Jets and a one-point loss in the final minute to Detroit, to leave the team with an 8-7 record. Only a season-salvaging win in the finale against Indianapolis allowed the Vikings to squeak into the playoffs. After so many years of playoff futility, little was expected when the Vikings went to New York to play the Giants. But, with Johnson down with injury, the Vikings rallied around backup Randall Cunningham to score 13 fourth-quarter points for an improbable 23-22 win over the NFC East champion Giants—giving Green his first playoff win in five tries, but giving the team a date with San Francisco.

The 49ers dispatched the Vikings in short order, building a 24-7 lead midway through the third quarter on their way to a 38-22 win. The loss again left people questioning Green's future with the team. Instead, it would be the organization that would change, not the head coach.

In January, 1998, Viking President Roger Headrick was convinced he would be the man to lead a group to buy the Vikings. Instead, author Tom Clancy led a group that offered $200 million for the team—an offer accepted by the Viking owners. In subsequent weeks, the Vikings, known league wide as one of the stingier teams, spent $80 million to make sure that John Randle, Todd Steussie and Robert Smith remained in the fold with other long-term signers Brad Johnson, Cris Carter, Jake Reed and Randall McDaniel.

Clancy's deal would eventually fall apart, opening the door for San Antonio billionaire Red McCombs to buy the team for $250 million, promising "to restore Purple Pride" to the Minnesota Vikings and bring back an excitement that has been missing for a decade.

Much like Vikings teams of 25 years earlier, the Vikings realize that their dream of a Super Bowl title may still be on the horizon. There is a finite window of opportunity for it to happen, but heading into the 1998 season, the Vikings are confident that the future isn't as far off as it may appear and the glory days for the Vikings may loom ahead instead of fading away in scrapbooks.

TRIVIA QUESTIONS

1. With the removal of Mike Lynn and the takeover bid of Irwin Jacobs and Carl Pohlad thwarted, the Vikings had a 10-member board of directors that ran the team for six years. How many of those 10 owners can you name?

2. In 1973, Dennis Green got his coaching start as a running backs and receivers coach at which university?

3. In 1981, he took over a program notorious for losing and helped turn it around. What university gave Green his first head coaching job?

4. In his second year at that school, he stopped a long losing streak with a win over Northern Illinois. How many games in a row had that team lost?

5. In 1986, he left the college game to be an assistant at San Francisco. What was his capacity as an assistant coach?

6. Green returned to head coaching in college in 1989. What college did he go to?

7. In 1990, his college team beat the No. 1 ranked team in the country on the road. What team was that?

8. In his final season at that school, he was close to bringing in a disgruntled player from a top-10 college program who had quit the team because of his coach's lack of commitment to academics. Who was this player?

9. When Green came to Minnesota, how many of his starters were 30

years of age or older?

10. Five years later, how many of his starters were 30 or older?

11. In 1992, in how many games did the Viking defense allow the opponents to score 20 points or less?

12. In that season, how many times did the Viking offense score 21 points or more?

13. The Vikings 21-20 win over Chicago was memorable because it was the Monday night game in which Mike Ditka went berserk with quarterback Jim Harbaugh for an interception that was returned for a touchdown that turned the game around in Minnesota's favor. Who made that big interception?

14. Who was the only Central Division team to beat the Vikings in 1992?

15. In 1992, the Vikings played two games where the winning team did not score a touchdown—winning one and losing one. Who did the Vikings beat without scoring a TD and who did they lose to?

16. In the Vikings' 1992 playoff loss to Washington, the Vikings took an early 7-0 lead before surrendering the final 24 points. Who scored Minnesota's touchdown on the game's opening drive?

17. The Redskins got a 100-yard rushing performance from an unlikely source in that game. Who gave the Redskin offense a boost?

18. The Redskins scored three touchdowns to blow out the Vikings. Who scored them?

19. Of the 60 minutes of that game, what was the time of possession enjoyed by the Vikings?

20. Following the first drive of the game, how many yards did Sean Salisbury throw for in that game?

21. In 1993, the Vikings recorded two shutouts. What two teams did they blank?

22. What was memorable about the shutout that happened at the Metrodome?

23. When was the last time prior to 1993 that the Viking defense had two shutouts in one year?

24. In 1993, how many times did the Vikings score more than 21 points in a game?

25. Although he never put up spectacular numbers, Jim McMahon was known simply for winning games. In his one season as a starter for the Vikings, what was his regular season record in games he started?

26. In the 1993 playoffs against the Giants, what was the score at halftime?

27. What Giant scored two touchdowns in the second half to help bury the Vikings?

28. Who led the Vikings in tackles in 1993—the second of three straight years he would lead the team?

29. How was the player mentioned above acquired by the Vikings?

30. In 1993, this Viking led the team in punt returns, but may be best remembered for hauling in a 50-yard pass in the closing seconds of a home game that same year that allowed the Vikings to beat the up-and-coming Packers. Who was he?

31. 1993 was the last season for this Viking punter, who led the NFC in punting average two different seasons while in Minnesota?

32. In his 11 starts with the Vikings, how many touchdowns did Jim McMahon throw?

33. With Terry Allen down with a knee injury, this Viking led the team with 488 yards rushing—which ranked him only 34th in the NFL. Who was he?

34. On April 14, 1994, the Vikings traded two draft picks to Houston to acquire Warren Moon. What picks were they?

35. Who did those two players end up being that Houston obtained for Moon?

36. Who was the quarterback that had the Oilers confident in peddling Moon?

37. When the Vikings started the 1994 season with a 7-2 record, who were the only two teams to beat them?

38. In a four-game span from November 12 to December 1, 1994, the Vikings played three overtime games. Who did they play and what was the outcome?

39. What was the Vikings' home record in 1994?

40. Brad Johnson had been listed as the No. 2 quarterback all season for the Vikings in 1994. But, when Warren Moon went down with an injury before the season finale against the 49ers, who started that game?

41. The Vikings assumed in their playoff game with the Bears that they would have the quarterback advantage even with Moon hobbled, but the Chicago QB threw a pair of touchdowns. Who was this quarterback and who caught his touchdown passes?

42. The Bears also had two touchdown runs in the game. What backs scored for Chicago that day?

43. Warren Moon was able to rally the Vikings for two touchdowns. Who was on the receiving end of those passes?

44. Moon set a Viking playoff record for yards passing that day. How

many yards did he throw for?

45. One player accounted for more than half of those yards. Who set the record for most receptions in a playoff game that day and had the second-highest yardage total in Viking playoff history?

46. The Vikings were victims of costly turnovers and penalties in the loss. How many turnovers and penalties did the Vikings have that day?

47. This Viking was the sole sack leader for the team in 1994, the first time he led the team by himself. Who was he?

48. These two Vikings tied for the team lead in interceptions in 1994. Ironically, neither would be with the team in 1995. Who were they?

49. Fuad Reveiz led the NFC in scoring in 1994 and tied a Vikings' single-season record that year. How many points did Reveiz score?

50. In 1994, Warren Moon became the first Viking to top 4,000 yards passing in a season. Whose Viking record did he break and what season had the previous record been set?

51. Terry Allen was only the third Viking to top 1,000 yards rushing in a season, joining Chuck Foreman and Ted Brown. Between the three of them, how many 1,000-yard seasons did they have?

52. In Green's first three years, what was his regular-season record in six games against the Packers? The Bears? The Lions? The Buccaneers?

53. In 1995, the Vikings scored 40 or more points twice, for the first time since 1988. Against what two teams did the Vikings light up the scoreboard?

54. In how many games in 1995 did the Viking defense, renowned for its ability to keep teams off the scoreboard in the '90s, allow 20 or more points?

55. What was the Vikings' road record in 1995?

56. During the 1995 season, a key component to the Vikings' glory years success was elected into the Pro Football Hall of Fame. Who was he?

57. In 1995, this player became only the third rookie in Viking history to lead the team in interceptions. Who was he and who were the other two Viking rookies to lead the team in picks?

58. The 1995 interception leader in the last question made history for the Vikings that year. What was his accomplishment?

59. In 1995, this Viking punt returner brought a punt back 74 yards for a touchdown, becoming only the fourth Viking to ever return a punt for a touchdown. Who was he and who were the other three?

60. Also in 1995, Qadry Ismail came close to becoming only the third Viking to return a kickoff for a touchdown—being tripped up on the 10-yard line. Who would he have joined as the only Vikings to return a kickoff for a touchdown?

61. In 1995, Warren Moon set a Viking record for touchdown passes. How many did Moon throw that year and whose record did he break?

62. On July 26, 1996, the Vikings lost one of the main forces in bringing Minnesota NFL football and Super Bowl XXVI. What famous Minnesota sports figure died that day?

63. The Vikings started 1996 with a 4-0 record. When was the last time the Vikings had begun a season with four wins?

64. Minnesota had four games blacked out locally during the 1996 season. What was their record in those games the home fans didn't see?

65. What was their home record in the four games the home fans saw on TV?

66. In 1996, the Vikings beat the Carolina Panthers, leaving only two NFL franchises the Vikings haven't defeated. They are both on the 1998 schedule. Who are they?

67. With Warren Moon injured, Brad Johnson got the call as the starting quarterback. He had played the previous spring in another league, where he earned his bone as an NFL quarterback. With what team did he spend his spring with in 1995?

68. In the Vikings' playoff game with Dallas, the Cowboys took control early. What was the score at halftime of the 40-15 loss?

69. This Cowboy player was instrumental in the blowout, stripping Amp Lee of an apparent game-tying TD early, forcing a Leroy Hoard fumble that led to a Cowboy touchdown one play later and scoring one on an interception. Who was he?

70. The Vikings scored two touchdowns in the game. Who scored them?

71. The Dallas game also marked the first time the Vikings scored a two-point conversion in the playoffs. How did they score?

72. In the 1997 season, the Vikings started the year 8-2, including a six-game winning streak. When was the last time the Vikings had won six games in a row?

73. The winning streak was coincided with the publication of Denny Green's book. What was the title of that book?

74. Who co-wrote the book with Green?

75. After the 8-2 start, the Vikings lost five straight games. When was the last time a Viking team had a longer losing streak than that?

76. Green finally earned his first playoff win against the Giants December 27, 1997. But he needed some divine intervention. How many points did the Vikings score late and how long did it take?

77. What was the score at halftime of that game?

78. What was the frustrating part of that score from the New York perspective?

79. Who scored the Vikings' first touchdown of the game?

80. Trailing, 22-13, with less than two minutes to play, who scored a touchdown to get the Vikings within two points?

81. The ensuing on-side kick looked to be recovered by the Giants, but it bounced off the chest of a New York player and into the arms of a Viking. Who mishandled the kick and who recovered it?

82. Veteran kicker Eddie Murray hit the game-winning field goal. How many previous playoff game-winners had Murray notched over his career?

83. The following week, the Vikings fell behind, 21-7, to the 49ers after San Francisco scored 14 points in 47 seconds. Who scored the 49ers' two touchdowns?

84. Minnesota ended up scoring three touchdowns in the game. Who scored them?

85. This running back rolled for 125 yards in the game. Who was he?

86. This Viking caught five passes for 114 yards to be the game's leading yardage receiver. Who was he?

87. In the 49er game, Cunningham set a Minnesota playoff milestone. What record had no Viking quarterback accomplished in 31 previous playoff games?

88. Following the 1997 season, author Tom Clancy led a group that signed a purchase agreement with the Vikings. How much did the group shell out to buy the Vikings?

89. Less than Six months later, the team was sold to Red McCombs. How much did he pay for the franchise?

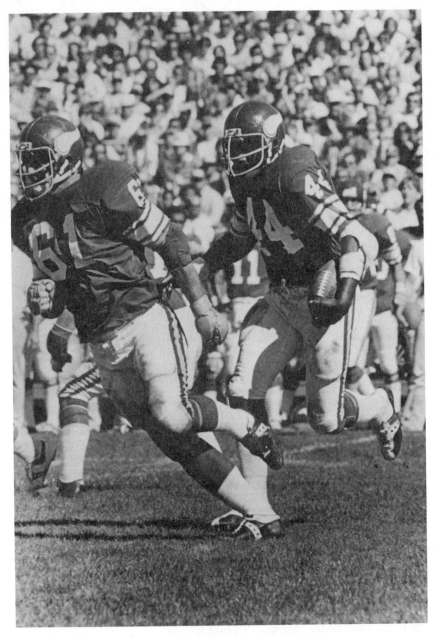

Chuck Foreman runs behind his blockers.

9

BY THE NUMBERS

O ver the years, more than 1,000 players have donned the Viking colors— some for many years and others for only a pre-season game or two. Here's a chance to test your knowledge of the numbers that made the Viking players famous and infamous.

TRIVIA QUESTIONS

1. Who are the only two Vikings to have their numbers retired?

2. While every number from 1 to 99 has been worn by Viking players, only two numbers have been worn by a single player. One makes sense and one doesn't. Who were the players and what were their numbers?

3. Running back Robert Smith wore two different numbers in his Viking career. What were those two numbers?

4. One player holds the distinction of wearing four different jersey numbers as a member of the Vikings. Who was that player?

5. Several numbers have been worn by less than a handful of players,

but one number has been worn by many more than any other issued. What is the number and how many different players have worn it?

6. Two numbers have been worn by players with the same last name. What are the numbers and the players who wore them? Hint: both sets of players played the same position.

7. Who was the first Viking to wear a single-digit number?

8. Four Vikings have been able to claim "I'm No. 1" because they wore No. 1—including three high-scoring kickers. Name the three players?

9. Three other kickers—both known for their field goal prowess—were the only players issued No. 3 with the Vikings. Name them.

10. Two quarterbacks in team history have worn No. 7. One of them was the replacement quarterback during the Vikings' strike debacle team in 1987 and the other was the quarterback who led the Vikings to their first road playoff win since the 1987 season. Who are they?

11. Prior to 1997 rookie quarterback Todd Bouman being issued his college No. 8, only one Viking had ever worn that number. Who was it?

12. Fran Tarkenton wasn't the only Viking to wear No. 10. There was one other. Who was he?

13. Two Viking quarterbacks that were named team M.V.P. both wore No. 11. Who were they?

14. The Vikings first starting quarterback, their quarterback of the future and their all-time leading scorer all wore No. 14. Who are they?

15. Two quarterbacks were the only Vikings ever given the No. 16. Who were they?

16. Aside from Bobby Bryant, the No. 20 has been worn by three running backs that have been team leaders in rushing. Who are the three backs?

backs?

17. 10 different players have worn No. 22 over the years, but one wore it for 12 seasons and made it synonymous with him. Who was he?

18. Nine players have worn No. 28, but one, who was acquired in a trade for reserve defensive lineman Bob Lurtsema, is unquestionably the most famous. Who was he?

19. Only five players have ever worn No. 30, because one player owned the number for 13 years. Who was he?

20. What future Hall of Famer once wore No. 33 with the Vikings?

21. Only three Vikings have ever worn No. 38. One was 1987 replacement scab Fletcher Louallen, but the other two are much better remembered. Can you name the hard-hitting safety that starred in the early 1990s and the tight end that played with Fran Tarkenton in both Minnesota and New York?

22. What a difference a number can make. Both of these players wore No. 42. One was acquired cheaply in a trade and went on to be one of the best wide receivers of the 1970s and the other was the highest running back selected by Minnesota in the last 15 years and was a two-sport bust. Can you name them?

23. Surprisingly, 11 players have worn No. 53. Why is that surprising? Because one player wore it for 17 years. Who was he?

24. Two of the Vikings leading tacklers at middle linebacker shared the No. 55. Can you name these ball hawks of the 1980s and 1990s?

25. Two of the Vikings most durable guards have shared the No. 64. Name them.

26. One of the original Vikings, this player wore No. 67 for 14 years. Who was he?

27. Two All-Pro offensive tackles have helped assure that a scant few Vikings players have ever worn No. 73. Who are they?

28. The player who caught the first touchdown in Viking history and the one who caught the most both wore No. 80. Name them.

29. Two players of very different styles wore No. 81. One was a cornerstone of the Purple People Eater defense, while the other once held nearly every receiving record in team history. Who are they?

30. Prior to Cris Carter's 17 touchdowns in 1995, this was the last Viking receiver to score double digit touchdowns and made No. 85 show up on a lot of highlight films. Who was he?

31. In a related question, the answer to No. 30 was only the second Viking to score 10 or more TDs in a season. This player, who wore No. 89, scored 11 in the Vikings first season—a record that stood until Carter broke it in '95. Who was he?

32. Defensive tackle John Randle has made No. 93 a popular number. He is only the second Viking to ever wear it. Who was the first?

33. Only three players have ever worn No. 97 for the Vikings. Two—Jose White and Tony Norman—were forgettable. But one made major impact as an immovable defensive lineman for the Vikings. Who was he?

MATCHING

Match the following players with the number they wore with the Vikings:

1. Terry Allen	A. 7
2. Ted Brown	B. 9
3. Joey Browner	C. 21
4. Chris Doleman	D. 23
5. Paul Flatley	E. 29
6. Chuck Foreman	F. 39
7. Wally Hilgenberg	G. 44
8. Karl Kassaulke	H. 47
9. Gary Larsen	I. 50
10. Hugh McElhenny	J. 56
11. Jim McMahon	K. 58
12. Keith Millard	L. 62
13. Fuad Reveiz	M. 75
14. Joe Senser	N. 77
15. Jeff Siemon	O. 81
16. Gene Washington	P. 84
17. Ed White	Q. 85

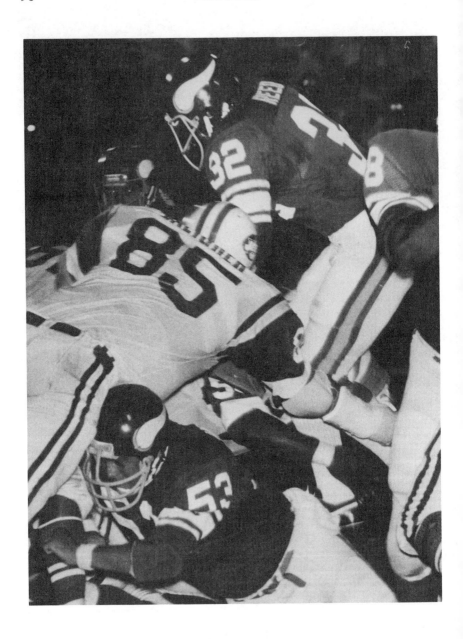

Oscar Reed drives into the pile against the New York Jets.

10

MINNESOTA'S ON THE CLOCK

Every year, NFL teams look at the annual college draft to build their teams and set the tone for the future of the franchise. Few teams, however, can boast the number of late-round gems that the Vikings have pulled out through the years. While some of the top picks have been hit-and-miss duds, Minnesota scouting gurus Frank Gilliam and Jerry Reichow have culled some impressive talent that have become stars in the annals of Vikings history. See how you do in answering the following questions about the diamonds in the rough and the lumps of coal pulled out when the Vikings have been on the clock for the NFL draft.

TRIVIA QUESTIONS

1. Most Vikings fans know that in the 1961 draft the Vikings acquired Tommy Mason, Rip Hawkins and Fran Tarkenton. But on the fifth round that year, they drafted a defensive back who would remain with the team until 1972. Who was he?

2. In the fourth round of the 1962 draft, the Vikings drafted a linebacker that later had his own theme song because he "hits good like a linebacker should." Who was he?

3. In the 1963 draft, the Vikings picked this University of Minnesota player on the second round, but he decided against playing for the Vikings, instead opting for the AFL. He went on to go to the Hall of Fame. Name him.

4. In 1963, the Vikings traded away a sixth-round pick to get some also-rans from the Cleveland Browns. One of those players went on to play for the Vikings for 15 years. Who was he?

5. In 1964, the Vikings drafted another University of Minnesota standout. He stayed with the team and became a fixture. Can you name him?

6. The Vikings traded their fourth-round pick in the 1964 draft to get running back Bill Brown. To what team did the Vikings trade that pick?

7. In 1965, the Vikings drafted two players who went on to become household names with the Los Angeles Rams. One never signed with the Vikings. The other did, but enjoyed some of his best days in L.A. Do you know who they are?

8. On the 13th round of the 1965 draft, the Vikings drafted a native of Cando, North Dakota, who had a long career with Minnesota. Who was he?

9. On the 14th round of the 1966 draft, the Vikings selected a tight end from Tulsa who never played with Minnesota, but went on to earn a pair of Super Bowl rings. Can you name him?

10. In 1967, the Vikings had three first-round picks, each of whom became key cogs to Vikings glory days to come. Can you name them in the order they were drafted?

11. On the seventh round of the 1967 draft, the Vikings plucked a cornerback who would also become a regular starter. Can you name him?

12. In the 1968 draft, the Vikings got the No. 1 pick in the draft as part

of the Fran Tarkenton trade? Whom did they select?

13. In 1969, the year the Vikings went to their first Super Bowl, the draft was almost a complete dud. Only one player stuck with the team beyond that season, but he became a stalwart on the offensive line. Who was he?

14. On the 10th round of the 1970 draft, the Vikings took a tight end from Wisconsin who became known for being a glue-fingered receiver. Name him.

15. In 1971, the Vikings used their top pick to take a running back from Ohio State they hoped would give the rushing game a boost. Who was he?

16. In 1971, the Vikings got a pick from New England as part of the Joe Kapp trade that helped solidify an already strong defense. Who was this player?

17. When the Vikings traded quarterback Gary Cuozzo to the Cardinals, they got a second-round draft pick and a player. Who were these two players?

18. In the 1973 draft, the Vikings again made a pitch for running backs, using their first- and fifth-round picks on rushers. They both made an impact. Can you name them?

19. In 1974, the Vikings had two picks in each of the first three rounds. In the first two rounds, they selected a pair of linebackers. Name them.

20. In 1975 and 1976, the Vikings used their top picks to draft defensive linemen to eventually replace the Purple People Eaters. Can you name these two?

21. In the second round of the 1976 draft, the Vikings went to Grambling —a college that would later bring them Jake Reed—to get a wide receiver. Who was the player they got in 1976?

22. In 1977, the Vikings drafted two players that would be the

cornerstones of the offense and defense for the next decade. One was taken on the first round, while the other was scooped on the ninth round. Can you name them?

23. In 1978, the Vikings again tried their hand at drafting a defensive lineman, with mixed success. Who was this latest attempt to return the Purple People Eaters to past glory?

24. In 1979, the Vikings drafted their next running back of the future. Who was he?

25. In 1980, the Vikings used a defensive lineman with their first pick for the fourth time in six years. Who was he?

26. The Vikings traded away their first-round pick in the 1981 draft to acquire two second-rounders from the Colts. In all, the Vikes had three picks in the second round that year. Who did they select?

27. In the third round that same year, the Vikings acquired a third-round pick from New England for Chuck Foreman. What offensive lineman did they draft with that pick?

28. On the eighth round of the 1981 draft, the Vikings selected a player who was both a quarterback and punter. Who was he?

29. In 1982, the Vikings drafted a University of Minnesota linebacker who never made the team. He eventually stuck in the NFL and earned two Super Bowl rings. Who was he?

30. On the first round of the 1982 draft, the Vikings picked running back Darrin Nelson out of Stanford. What three running backs went later in the draft that year?

31. In the 23rd year of Vikings history, the team finally drafted a defensive back with its first pick in the draft in 1983. Who was it?

32. Later in the same draft, the Vikings took another defensive back on the seventh round. Name him.

33. In the 1984 and 1985 drafts, the Vikings selected players who would eventually become defensive icons. One didn't sign—opting for the USFL before it went belly up—and the other was drafted as a linebacker, but moved to the defensive line. Who were these two players?

34. The 1985 draft also produced a pair of players that would have productive careers—both enjoying excellent seasons and better money away from Minnesota. Can you name the center the Vikings took on the third round and the quarterback they took on the sixth round that year?

35. The Vikings again tried to draft a defensive lineman with their top pick in 1986. Who was this Auburn product?

36. The Vikings didn't have a No. 2 pick in 1986, because they traded it to the New York Giants for this USFL player. Who was this player the Giants weren't enamored with?

37. The Vikings traded a No. 2 pick to Miami in 1986 to get another USFL product. Who was he?

38. Looking for help at running back in 1987, the Vikings drafted a two-sport athlete with their top pick—one whose first sport obviously wasn't football. Who was he?

39. On the third round of the 1987 draft, the Vikings took a defensive lineman from Louisiana State who they hoped would be a roster filler. He became more than that. Who was he?

40. In 1988, the Vikings drafted both of the starting guards from Arizona State—one on the first round and one on the fourth. Who were they?

41. That same year, the Vikings traded away a fourth- and 11th-round pick to get this player from New England. Who was he?

42. The Vikings set a record of sorts in the 1988 draft. They did something that year they haven't done before or since. What did they do … or not do?

43. From 1990 to 1992 the Vikings didn't have first-round picks because of the Herschel Walker trade. But they didn't have a first-round pick in 1989, either, because they traded it away for a veteran player. Who did they trade the pick to and who did they acquire?

44. The Vikings didn't have their top two picks in 1990, but still added two key players. One was a promising back they took in the ninth round and the other was an undrafted free agent defensive player. Can you name these two?

45. In 1991 and 1995, the Vikings used draft picks to select defensive backs from Southwest Louisiana State. Can you name these two players?

46. In the 1992 draft, the Vikings drafted defensive end Robert Harris in the second round in a trade with Seattle. Who did the Vikings send to the Seahawks to get the pick?

47. The gems of the 1992 draft came later. In the fifth round and the ninth rounds, the Vikings took a chance on a pair of players whom they hoped would develop as projects with the team. Both did. Who did the Vikings take the fliers on?

48. In 1993, the Vikings had their first pick in the opening round in five years. Who did they select with that pick?

49. A trade with Denver in 1994 helped the Vikings get two first-round draft picks. Who did the Vikings take with those two picks?

50. Another trade that included Denver gave the Vikings two first-round picks in the 1995 draft. Who did the Vikings take that season?

51. In 1996 and 1997, the Vikings used their top pick to take a linebacker. Who were these top draftees?

11

FOR THE RECORD

T he Vikings have had some impressive team and individual accomplishments since joining the NFL. While other franchises had a big head start on them, the Vikings have found their way into the NFL record books for several team and individual accomplishments.

See if you can match the Vikings buried in the voluminous pages of NFL lore with the records they set.

TRIVIA QUESTIONS

1. When the Vikings made the Herschel Walker trade in 1989, it set a record for the most players and draft picks that changed hands in one deal. How many different players were eventually impacted by the trade that brought Walker to the Vikings?

2. Since the NFL merger in 1970, the Vikings have won 12 division titles. What teams have won more?

3. Since the merger, the Vikings have made 18 playoff appearances. How many teams have made more?

4. When Fran Tarkenton was elected to the Hall of Fame in 1986, what four other players were inducted with him?

5. When Alan Page went to the Hall of Fame in 1988, three other football legends went in with him. Who were they?

6. When Paul Krause was voted into the Hall of Fame in 1998, he was one of five inductees. Can you name the other four?

7. What is the Vikings' record in NFL/NFC title games?

8. In the Pro Bowl in January, 1965, what Viking won the honor of Outstanding Back?

9. In the Pro Bowl in January, 1979, a Viking was named the game's M.V.P. Who was he?

10. That Pro Bowl was significant for a locational reason. What made that game one worthy of being a trivia question?

11. The Vikings have made a pair of NFL transatlantic firsts in playing games overseas. On August 6, 1983, the Vikings beat the St. Louis Cardinals, 28-10, in the first NFL game ever played in this city. What city was it?

12. The Vikings had another first when they beat Chicago, 28-21, August 14, 1988, in this city. Where was this game played?

13. To date, the Vikings are 4-0 playing games outside the United States. What other two foreign cities did the Vikings play in and whom did they beat?

14. Through the 1997 season, what was the Vikings' record on Monday Night Football?

15. In this season, the Vikings played on Monday night three times. What year was that?

16. In only four seasons have the Vikings not played a Monday night game. What years were they?

17. The Vikings have played at least one game on Monday night every year since 1987. Only two teams have a longer string of consecutive seasons with a game in the national prime-time spotlight. Who are they?

18. On one Monday night game, the Vikings defense surrendered an NFL record that will never be broken. Why? Because it can't be broken —only tied. What record is that?

19. This player set a record for most catches (14), most yards (289) and most touchdowns (3) in a Monday night game against the Vikings December 18, 1995. Who is he?

20. Eddie Anderson of the Raiders holds the record for longest interception for a touchdown return in Monday Night Football history with a 102-yard return vs. Miami. But this Viking is second all time. He took a pick back 94 yards against Chicago December 19, 1988. Who was he?

21. Little known Harold Hart of Oakland took a kickoff back 102 yards for a touchdown to set an Monday Night Football record. This Viking is second. Who was he, how long was his kickoff return and against what team did he have the coast-to-coast return?

22. Since overtime was brought back in 1974, how many overtime games have the Vikings had and where does that rank them among the NFL leaders?

23. What is the Vikings record in overtime games?

24. In two different seasons the Vikings had four overtime games. In what years were they?

25. That fell one short of the NFL record of five in one year. Which team went to OT five times in 1983?

26. Three overtime games in NFL history have been decided by a fake field goal converted into a touchdown. Ironically, the Vikings have been involved in all three. What team did they beat with a fake field goal pass, what team beat them with a pass and what team beat them with a run out of a fake field goal?

27. The longest pass for a touchdown to win an overtime game was a 99-yarder from Ron Jaworski to Mike Quick in 1988, but the next three longest belong to the Vikings. Who were the tandems that hooked up for these three 50-plus yard TD passes to end games?

28. When the NFL named its 75th anniversary team, only one player who wore a Viking uniform was a member of the team. Who was he?

29. The NFL named a 1970s All-Decade Team and two Vikings were on that list. Who were they?

30. Jim Marshall is one of a select few players to play 20 years in the NFL. Only two players have had longer stints in the NFL as active players. Who were they?

31. Two Vikings are Nos. 1 and 2 for consecutive games played in NFL history. Who were they and how many games made up their respective streaks?

32. Who was the only Viking to lead the NFL is scoring two different seasons?

33. This Viking kicker set the all-time NFL record for most consecutive extra points without a miss. Who was he and how many did he make before he finally missed one?

34. This Viking shares a record with two other NFL kickers for making seven field goals in a game. Who was the Viking, against what team did he accomplish this and who does he share the record with?

35. This Viking kicker set an NFL record for consecutive games with at least one field goal. Who was he and how many games in a row did he

kick a field goal?

36. This Viking kicker set an NFL record for most consecutive field goals made without a miss. Who was he and how many in a row did he make?

37. Two Vikings are tied for the NFL record for safeties in a season with two. One did it in 1971; the other in 1981. Who were they?

38. The NFL record for most passes attempted and completed in one game came against the Vikings November 13, 1994. Who was the quarterback and how many passes did he throw and complete?

39. Joe Kapp is tied for the NFL record of seven TD passes in one game with four other quarterbacks. How many of the others can you name?

40. This Vikings quarterback is No. 2 all-time for most passes attempted in a game without an interception—second only to the player mentioned above who set the record for most passes in one game. Who was the Viking at No. 2 and how many passes did he throw?

41. Cris Carter set a record in 1994 with 122 receptions. He matched that total in 1995, but lost the record by one to which receiver?

42. In 1995, Cris Carter scored 17 receiving touchdowns. Only three receivers in NFL history have caught more TDs in a season. Can you name them?

43. This former Viking is listed twice on the all-time top five list of players with interceptions in consecutive games. He picked off passes in seven straight games with another team and six straight with the Vikings. Who was he?

44. This Viking set an NFL record for 27 fair catches in 1989. Name him.

45. This Viking holds the NFL record for defensive fumble recoveries. Who was he and how many fumbles did he recover?

46. Two Vikings rate in the top three for fumble recoveries in a season. This player recovered nine in one year for the record and the other recovered seven. Who were these opportunistic players?

47. This Viking set an NFL record for a rookie with 1,345 punt return yards. Who was he?

48. The Vikings won six division titles from 1973-78. Only one team has won more consecutive divisional crowns. Who was it?

49. In 1981, the Vikings set an all-time NFL passing record. What record was it?

50. On November 12, 1967, the Viking defense forced a single-game NFL record number of fumbles by the Detroit Lions. How many times did Detroit cough up the ball?

51. In 1980, the Vikings offense essentially tied a record held by the 1938 Philadelphia Eagles—which played only 11 games. What record did the Vikings tie in a 16-game schedule that may never be broken?

52. In 1963, the Vikings set an NFL record for most fumbles forced in one year. How many fumbles did the Vikes recover that year in 14 games?

53. The Vikings led the NFL in fewest points allowed three straight seasons. What years were they?

54. In 1971, the Vikings set a modern-day record for least rushing touchdowns allowed. How many TDs did opposing runners score that year?

55. In 1989, the Vikings fell one short of the all-time NFL record for sacks. How many sacks did the Vikings have in '89 and what team beat them by one?

56. Chuck Foreman led the NFC in touchdowns for three straight years (1974-76). How many TDs did he score in those three seasons?

57. Three times Vikings quarterbacks have led the NFL in passer rating. Who were they and in what years did they do it?

58. Who was the last Viking to lead the NFL in rushing yardage?

59. Cris Carter led the NFL in receptions when he set a record with 122 in 1994. Was he the first Viking to lead the NFL in receptions in a season?

60. Who was the last Viking to lead the NFL in receiving yardage?

61. The Vikings have led the NFL in scoring only once. What year was it?

62. Bud Grant is No. 1 all-time for the Vikings in coaching wins. Who is No. 2?

63. Two Vikings players are tied for the team record of leading the Vikes in touchdowns five different seasons. Who were they?

64. This player scored touchdowns in seven consecutive games to set a team record. Who was he?

65. The longest field goal in Viking history is a 54-yarder. Who kicked it?

66. Chuck Foreman holds the Viking record for most rushing yards in one game. How many yards did he gain versus Philadelphia October 24, 1976?

67. Four opposing players have topped 200 yards rushing in a game against the Vikings. How many can you name?

68. What Viking holds the record for most 100-yard rushing games in a season with six?

69. Who holds the Vikings record for most 300-yard passing games in a season with six?

70. The longest completion in Vikings history was a pass play that covered 89 yards in a game against the Chicago Bears. Who was the tandem that set this record?

71. What Viking holds the record for most receptions in a game with 15?

72. What Viking receiver holds the team record for consecutive games with a reception?

73. Cris Carter and Jake Reed have combined to set what NFL record?

74. What Viking holds the record for most consecutive rushing attempts without a fumble?

75. Three players are tied for the Viking record of leading the team in interceptions four different seasons. Can you name these three amigos?

76. Who is the Viking career sack leader?

77. In 1989, this Viking came one sack short of the all-time NFL record for sacks in a season. Who was he, how many sacks did he have and whose record did he come close to?

78. Who holds the Vikings career record for blocked kicks?

79. Who holds the Viking record for most 300-yard games and what was his record in those games?

80. There is only one Viking with more than two 100-yard rushing games that never lost a game in which he topped the century mark. Who was it?

81. Throwing for 300 yards doesn't always mean you have a winning record in those games. In fact, only two Viking quarterbacks with more than one 300-yard game had winning records in those games. Who were they?

82. Only two Vikings with more than two 100-yard receiving games

never lost a game when they had 100 or more yards. Who were they?

83. As far as percentages go, this Viking was almost guaranteed money in the bank. When he caught for 100 or more yards, the Vikings had a 13-1 record. Who was he?

Ricky Young

Carl Eller

Ahmad Rashad

Jim Marshall

12

BIG MEN ON CAMPUS

P rior to coming to the NFL, almost every player was a standout at his college alma mater.

Here's a test of your memory of college players that went on to become Minnesota Vikings. See how many of these players you can correctly identify with the college at which they made a name for themselves.

TRIVIA QUESTIONS

1. Offensive tackle Grady Alderman

2. Defensive end Derrick Alexander

3. Running back Terry Allen

4. Linebacker Matt Blair

5. Running back Bill Brown

6. Running back Ted Brown

7. Safety Joey Browner

8. Cornerback Bobby Bryant

9. Wide receiver Anthony Carter

10. Wide receiver Cris Carter

11. Punter Greg Coleman

12. Running back Roger Craig

13. Kicker Rick Danmeier

14. Linebacker Jack Del Rio

15. Defensive tackle Paul Dickson

16. Defensive end Chris Doleman

17. Defensive end Carl Eller

18. Wide receiver Paul Flatley

19. Running back Chuck Foreman

20. Wide receiver John Gilliam

21. Safety Vencie Glenn

22. Linebacker Rip Hawkins

23. Linebacker Wally Hilgenberg

24. Offensive lineman David Huffman

25. Kicker Donald Igwebuike

26. Offensive tackle Tim Irwin

27. Quarterback Brad Johnson

28. Tight end Steve Jordan

29. Quarterback Joe Kapp

30. Defensive back Karl Kassaulke

31. Defensive tackle Gary Larsen

32. Cornerback Carl Lee

33. Center Kirk Lowdermilk

34. Defensive end Jim Marshall

35. Defensive end Doug Martin

36. Running back Tommy Mason

37. Offensive guard Randall McDaniel

38. Running back Hugh McElhenny

39. Quarterback Jim McMahon

40. Linebacker Fred McNeill

41. Defensive tackle Keith Millard

42. Quarterback Warren Moon

43. Defensive end Mark Mullaney

44. Running back Darrin Nelson

45. Running back Dave Osborn

46. Defensive tackle Alan Page

47. Defensive tackle John Randle

48. Wide receiver Ahmad Rashad

49. Wide receiver Jake Reed

50. Safety Todd Scott

51. Tight end Joe Senser

52. Defensive back Ed Sharockman

53. Linebacker Jeff Siemon

54. Offensive tackle Todd Steussie

55. Offensive tackle Korey Stringer

56. Linebacker Scott Studwell

57. Guard Milt Sunde

58. Defensive tackle Doug Sutherland

59. Quarterback Fran Tarkenton

60. Defensive tackle Henry Thomas

61. Center Mick Tingelhoff

62. Tight end Stu Voigt

63. Linebacker Lonnie Warwick

64. Wide receiver Gene Washington

65. Defensive back Charlie West

66. Offensive guard Ed White

67. Wide receiver Sammy White

68. Quarterback Wade Wilson

69. Linebacker Roy Winston

70. Defensive back Nate Wright

71. Offensive tackle Ron Yary

72. Offensive tackle Gary Zimmerman

Joe Senser

Keith Millard

Tommy Kramer

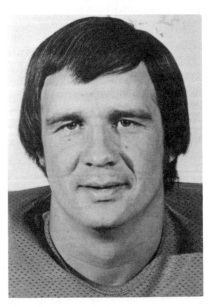

Paul Krause

13

AND THE WINNER IS ...

O ver the years, many Vikings have been recognized for individual achievement—during the successful years of the Vikings and through the lean years, too.

As Vikings fans can attest, several of the greatest players to take the field over the last four decades have worn purple and gold and, while the Hall of Fame has been slow to recognize them, their peers were not so jaded by the lack of a Super Bowl ring. Some may be surprised at how much the league's top hardware has been taken away by Vikings.

Here's a test of your knowledge of the honors and accolades earned by the Vikings.

TRIVIA QUESTIONS

1. The NFL has selected an All-Pro team since 1925. It isn't the same as the Pro Bowl, where two teams with reserves are selected. The All-Pro team is a single starting lineup. The Vikings didn't have a player named All-Pro until 1963. Who was that player?

2. From 1964 to 1967, this Viking was the only player selected All-Pro and he was also selected with others from 1968 to 1970. Who was he?

3. From 1968 to 1971, this defensive lineman was named All-Pro every year. Who was he?

4. In 1972, when the Vikings slipped to 7-7 there was only one player named to the NFL's All-Pro first team. Who was he?

5. How many consecutive years was the player mentioned above named to All-Pro teams?

6. For Vikings fans that contend that the hard-luck team of 1975 (the "Hail Mary" season) was the best the Vikings ever fielded got some support for their argument from the All-Pro selections. In 1975 a team-record six players were named All-Pro. Can you name that dirty half-dozen?

7. Following the Vikings' final Super Bowl appearance in 1976, the number of players on the All-Pro team dropped substantially. From 1977 to 1979, how many different Vikings were named to the All-Pro team?

8. The drought continued in the '80s until the Vikings made a late-season Super Bowl run in 1987. From 1980 to 1986, only two Vikings were named All-Pro. Name the players and the years they were selected?

9. From 1987 to 1990, one Viking was named to an All-Pro team each of those four years. Who was this defensive intimidator?

10. In 1991, only one Viking was named to the All-Pro team. Who was that player?

11. For more than two decades, Mick Tingelhoff stood alone at seven consecutive All-Pro team selections. Now two Vikings have current streaks that rival Tingelhoff. Who are those two players and, through the 1997 All-Pro selections, how many consecutive honors did they have?

12. In what years with the Vikings was Fran Tarkenton selected to the All-Pro team?

13. The Purple People Eaters will always be remembered among the

NFL's best defensive lines ever. Respectively, how many All-Pro nods were given to Alan Page, Carl Eller, and Jim Marshall?

14. Who was the only Viking punter named All-Pro and in what year did it happen?

15. Who was the only Viking kicker named All-Pro and what year did it happen?

16. The 1975 record of six All-Pro players was tied in 1992 when six players were selected. Think you can name those six?

17. Who were the only Vikings named NFL M.V.P. and what years were they selected?

18. *The Sporting News* hands out an award called "Executive of the Year." A Viking front office person won the honor once. Who was it?

19. On three occasions Vikings have been named NFL Defensive Player of the Year. Who were the players honored?

20. *Pro Football Weekly* hands out a series of awards each year including the "Comeback Player of the Year." Only one Viking has won that. Who was it and in what year did he win it?

21. Three Vikings have been named NFL Rookie of the Year. See if you can name the three players and the years in which they won the award?

22. The most unsung players in the league are offensive linemen, but an award called "The 1,000 Yard Club" honors the NFL's outstanding blocker. Can you name the two Vikings who won the award?

23. Two Vikings were selected to the Pro Bowl in the 1961 inaugural season. Who were they?

24. The first year the Vikings had a starter in the Pro Bowl was in 1963, when they had three. Can you name them?

25. Who was the first Viking picked to three straight Pro Bowls?

26. That record of three straight didn't last long, as a Viking would soon be selected to six straight Pro Bowls. Who was he?

27. Starting in 1968, how many consecutive years did the Vikings have a defensive lineman picked to the Pro Bowl?

28. On the subject of the Purple People Eaters defensive line, what was unique about the 1969 Pro Bowl?

29. Three Vikings defensive linemen started five or more Pro Bowls. Can you name them?

30. Of the Purple People Eaters, which of them was selected to the least number of Pro Bowls?

31. Twice during the Vikings' Super Bowl years six players were Pro Bowl starters—1969 and 1975. Who were the six starters in 1969?

32. In 1975, six Vikings started, but seven were selected as starters. Who were the six who played and the one who passed?

33. In the 1970s it became fashionable for star players to say "Thanks, but no thanks" to the Pro Bowl. Who was the first Vikings to turn down a trip to the Pro Bowl?

34. How many consecutive Pro Bowl starts did Ron Yary make?

35. In 1976, Fran Tarkenton turned down a trip to the Pro Bowl because he was busy doing something else that weekend. What was he doing?

36. From 1978 to 1981, only two Vikings played in the Pro Bowl and both were selected all four years. Can you name them?

37. In only one season did the Vikings have no players selected to the Pro Bowl. What year was that?

38. Who was the first Viking tight end picked to play in the Pro Bowl?

39. In 1982, 1984, and 1985, the Vikings sent only one player to the Pro Bowl and it wasn't the same player twice. Who was the player with each corresponding year?

40. The 1975 Viking team that had seven Pro Bowl starters selected also had two non-starters—Bobby Bryant and Paul Krause. In1988, the Vikings tied that record. Can you name the six starters and three reserves from that team?

41. When was the last time the Vikings didn't have an offensive lineman selected as a Pro Bowl starter?

42. How many consecutive years—thru 1997—has Randall McDaniel been selected as a Pro Bowl starter?

43. How many straight years—thru 1997—has John Randle been a Pro Bowl starter?

44. In the last 10 years, the Vikings have had only one quarterback, linebacker and kicker named to the Pro Bowl. Can you name all three?

45. In 1997, Randall McDaniel and Todd Steussie were both Pro Bowl starters on the offensive line. How many times have the Vikings had two offensive linemen start in the same season?

Chris Doleman

Cris Carter

Scott Studwell

Brad Johnson

14

THE END OF THE ROAD

In the current age of the NFL, free agency and salary caps have made player movement a common occurrence. The days of players like Jim Marshall playing for two decades with one team are a thing of the past. Either the player prices himself out of one market or another team covets him so much that he leaves his former team behind for greener pastures and thicker wallets elsewhere.

However, even back in the days when players were essentially slaves to an organization for their entire careers, some of the biggest names in the history of franchises moved on at the end of their playing days, as organizations gave up on the players before they gave up on their own NFL dreams. Vikings included on that list are some of the all-time greats, including Alan Page, Chuck Foreman, Carl Eller, Anthony Carter, Joey Browner, Tommy Kramer, Keith Millard, and Ron Yary.

The following list are all players who made an impact on the Minnesota Vikings, but ended their careers with other teams. Your job is to determine which team the player finished his career with. The only criterion here is the last team the player performed for during the regular season. Linebacker Jack Del Rio, for example, left the Vikings after the 1995 season and played for Miami in 1996, but was cut in the pre-season, so technically the NFL record books have his career ending in 1995 with the Vikings—since pre-season games don't count in official NFL statistics.

This could well be the "bar bet" section of this book because some of the answers may surprise you—even if you are a lifetime Viking fan who thought you knew everything there was to know about the purple and gold. See how many Viking heroes you can match with the teams they finished off their NFL careers with.

TRIVIA QUESTIONS

1. Defensive back Autry Beamon

2. Safety Joey Browner

3. Wide receiver Anthony Carter

4. Tight end Dave Casper

5. Punter Greg Coleman

6. Quarterback Gary Cuozzo

7. Quarterback Steve Dils

8. Running back D.J. Dozier

9. Defensive end Carl Eller

10. Wide receiver Paul Flatley

11. Running back Chuck Foreman

12. Wide receiver John Gilliam

13. Safety Vencie Glenn

14. Defensive back Dale Hackbart

15. Defensive back Issiac Holt

16. Offensive tackle Tim Irwin

17. Running back Clinton Jones

18. Wide receiver Hassan Jones

19. Quarterback Joe Kapp

20. Quarterback Tommy Kramer

21. Quarterback-punter Bob Lee

22. Cornerback Carl Lee

23. Running back Ed Marinaro

24. Running back Tommy Mason

25. Running back Hugh McElhenny

26. Defensive tackle Keith Millard

27. Defensive end Al Noga

28. Running back Dave Osborn

29. Defensive tackle Alan Page

30. Running back Oscar Reed

31. Kicker Benny Ricardo

32. Safety Todd Scott

33. Defensive tackle Doug Sutherland

34. Linebacker Lonnie Warwick

35. Wide receiver Gene Washington

36. Defensive back Charlie West

37. Offensive tackle Ed White

38. Guard Ron Yary

15

THIS, THAT, AND THE OTHER

B y this time, you should have a pretty good idea of the extent of your Viking trivia knowledge. But here is a final dose for you.

Unlike the other chapters, which ran along a similar theme or time frame, this final chapter of questions is a hodgepodge of past and current questions that just didn't get asked earlier in the book. Consider this the lightning round at the end of the game and test your skills at answering questions that have little or nothing in common with the question that preceded it.

TRIVIA QUESTIONS

1. What player did Bud Grant describe as the player that gave more on every down in every game?

2. What was Carl Eller's nickname?

3. Who wrote the "Skol Vikings" team rally song?

4. Where was Fran Tarkenton's home town?

5. Who has been the Vikings trainer since the beginning of the franchise?

6. Who was the Vikings highly-popular equipment man from the start of the franchise until the 1980s?

7. What was Joe Kapp's nickname?

8. Where was Mick Tingelhoff's home town?

9. What was Roy Winston's nickname?

10. Buster Rhymes used a nickname as opposed to his real first name. What was Buster's real first name?

11. In 1965, Paul Flatley had a record-setting day, catching eight passes for 200 yards and two touchdowns against San Francisco. What made the feat rather improbable?

12. Jim Marshall almost died at least three times during his playing career, but miraculously came away without a scratch in three serious situations. Can you name the three accidental ways Marshall cheated death while a Viking?

13. The low point of Jim Marshall's career had to be the wrong-way run of 1964. Here are a series of questions related to that incident. Who were the Vikings playing? Where was the game played? How far did he run? What player gave Marshall a big hug that made him realize he had run the wrong way?

14. What four Viking running backs have scored three touchdowns in one game?

15. What was Ahmad Rashad's given name?

16. What nickname was Karl Kassaulke given by Norm Van Brocklin and what did it mean?

17. What Viking defensive back was All-State in football and baseball as a Michigan high schooler and turned down a pro baseball contract to play football.

18. When the Vikings got Anthony Carter from the USFL, what team had he played for the previous season?

19. When the Vikings got Gary Zimmerman from the USFL, what team was he playing with?

20. This assistant coach served with Bud Grant both in Winnipeg and with the Vikings, coaching alongside Bud for 21 years. Who was he?

21. What was the name of Denny Green's band and what album did the band release in 1997 while Green was the Vikings' coach?

22. For years, the Vikings traveled the state of Minnesota with the Vikings Charity Basketball Team. What two players were credited as starting the team?

23. Vikings mascot Hub Meads became an icon on the Minnesota landscape, but, after his retirement, the Vikings brought in a drum-pounding lunatic who used to cheer on the Houston Oilers. What appropriate name did this cheerleader go by?

24. In the 1990s, the Vikings tried to return to a mascot that looked more like a Viking, while at the same time adding a cartoonish looking purple dinosaur that confounded fans about the relevance of dinosaurs and Vikings. Who was the human mascot and what was the name of the curiously-selected dinosaur?

25. What was Stu Voigt's nickname?

26. What Viking player didn't miss a game during the 1973 season, despite knowing that he would need cancer surgery following the season?

27. One of Mike Lynn's less-than-brilliant ideas was trying to form team

unity by spending almost $1 million to send the Vikings to a corporate teamwork-teaching facility in the southwestern United States. It turned out to be a joke to most of the players. What was the name of this summer camp?

28. What was defensive back Nate Allen's nickname?

29. In 1976, the start of the Vikings-Detroit game was delayed more than one-and-a-half hours. Why was is delayed?

30. From the NFL merger in 1970 to the completion of the 1997 season, what was the Vikings' record against the AFC?

31. When Mike Lynn left the Vikings in 1991, it wasn't on the best of terms. What was his severance cut the team gave him to get rid of him?

32. Where did the Vikings find Scottie Graham when they brought him to the team?

33. For a decade, Leo Lewis was a Viking regular. What made his long career with the Vikings a fluke?

34. What author, known for writing a book in which the Vikings actually won the Super Bowl, led a group of investors that signed a purchase agreement to buy the Vikings in 1998, only to have the bid fall through?

16

FROM THE HOME OFFICE

W hether it's radio disc jockeys or David Letterman, it seems everyone keeps track of Top 10 lists and the Vikings are no exception. There is a statistic for just about every aspect of the game and where there are stats, there are bound to be Top 10 lists. With that in mind, here are the top 10 in several major historical categories, combining players from different eras for the purpose of comparison.

Service (Career Games Played)

Rank	Player	Seasons	Games
1.	Jim Marshall	1961-79	270
2.	Mick Tingelhoff	1962-78	240
3.	Fred Cox	1963-77	210
4.	Carl Eller	1964-78	209
5.	Scott Studwell	1977-90	202
6.	Ron Yary	1968-82	199
7.	Grady Alderman	1961-74	194
8.	Roy Winston	1962-76	190
9.	Tim Irwin	1981-93	188
10.	Bill Brown	1962-74	182

Service (Career Starts)

Rank	Player	Seasons	Starts
1.	Jim Marshall	1961-79	270
2.	Mick Tingelhoff	1962-78	240
3.	Carl Eller	1964-78	209
4.	Tim Irwin	1981-93	181
5.	Ron Yary	1968-82	180
6.	Grady Alderman	1961-74	180
7.	Fran Tarkenton	1961-68, 1972-78	178
8(t).	Alan Page	1967-78	160
8(t).	Scott Studwell	1977-90	160
8(t).	Roy Winston	1962-76	160

Passing (Career)

Rank	Player	Seasons	Att-Com	Yds.	TD	Int.
1.	Fran Tarkenton	1961-66 1972-78	4,569-2,635	33,098	239	194
2.	Tommy Kramer	1977-89	3,648-2,011	24,775	159	157
3.	Wade Wilson	1981-91	1,665-929	12,135	66	75
4.	Warren Moon	1994-96	1,454-882	10,102	58	42
5.	Rich Gannon	1987-92	1,003-561	6,457	40	36
6.	Brad Johnson	1992-97	836-517	5,716	37	24
7.	Joe Kapp	1967-69	669-351	4,807	37	47
8.	Steve Dils	1979-83	623-336	3,867	15	18
9.	Gary Cuozzo	1968-71	556-276	3,552	18	23
10.	Sean Salisbury	1990-94	404-228	2,772	14	9

Passing (Season)

Rank	Player	Seasons	Att-Com	Yds.	TD	Int.
1.	Warren Moon	1994	601-337	4,264	18	19
2.	Warren Moon	1995	606-377	4,228	33	14
3.	Tommy Kramer	1980	593-322	3,912	26	24
4.	Tommy Kramer	1980	522-299	3,582	19	23
5.	Tommy Kramer	1985	506-277	3,522	19	26
6.	Fran Tarkenton	1978	572-345	3,468	25	32
7.	Tommy Kramer	1979	566-315	3,397	23	24
8.	Brad Johnson	1997	452-275	3,036	20	12
9.	Tommy Kramer	1986	372-208	3,000	24	10
10.	Fran Tarkenton	1975	425-273	2,994	25	13

Passing (Career)

Rank	Player	Att-Com	Yds.	TD	Opp./Date
1.	Tommy Kramer	35-20	490	3	at Washington * 11-2-1986
2.	Tommy Kramer	49-38	456	4	Cleveland * 12-14-1980
3.	Joe Kapp	43-28	449	7	Baltimore Colts * 9-28-1969
4.	Tommy Kramer	43-27	444	4	at San Diego * 10-11-1981
5.	Tommy Kramer	55-28	436	3	Chicago Bears * 9-19-1985
6.	Warren Moon	57-33	420	3	New Orleans * 11-6-1994
7.	Fran Tarkenton	34-21	407	3	at San Francisco * 10-24-1965
8.	Warren Moon	50-33	400	2	New York Jets * 11-20-1994
9.	Tommy Kramer	42-30	395	3	Atlanta * 9-7-1980
10.	Wade Wilson	35-28	391	2	Detroit * 11-6-1988

300-Yard Passing Games (Career)

Rank	Player	Seasons	Total
1.	Tommy Kramer	1977-89	19
2.	Warren Moon	1994-96	10
3.	Fran Tarkenton	1961-66, 1972-78	9
4.	Wade Wilson	1981-91	7
5.	Steve Dils	1979-83	3
6(t).	Brad Johnson	1992-97	2
6(t).	Rich Gannon	1987-92	2
6(t).	Sean Salisbury	1990-94	2
9.	Joe Kapp	1967-69	1

Rushing (Career)

Rank	Player	Seasons	Att.	Yds.	Ave.	TD
1.	Chuck Foreman	1973-79	1,529	5,879	3.8	52
2.	Bill Brown	1962-74	1,627	5,757	3.5	52
3.	Ted Brown	1979-86	1,117	4,546	4.1	40
4.	Warren Moon	1994-96	1,172	4,320	3.7	29
5.	Rich Gannon	1987-92	981	4,231	4.3	18
6.	Brad Johnson	1992-97	761	3,252	4.3	28
7.	Joe Kapp	1967-69	644	3,095	4.8	17
8.	Steve Dils	1979-83	641	2,795	4.4	23
9.	Gary Cuozzo	1968-71	453	2,543	5.6	22
10.	Sean Salisbury	1990-94	626	2,374	3.8	22

Rushing (Season)

Rank	Player	Season	Att.	Yds.	Ave.	TD
1.	Robert Smith	1997	232	1,266	5.5	6
2.	Terry Allen	1992	266	1,201	4.5	13
3.	Chuck Foreman	1976	278	1,155	4.1	13
4.	Chuck Foreman	1977	270	1,112	4.1	6
5.	Chuck Foreman	1975	280	1,070	3.8	13
6.	Ted Brown	1981	274	1,063	3.9	6
7.	Terry Allen	1994	255	1,031	4.0	8
8.	Dave Osborn	1967	215	972	4.5	2
9.	Ted Brown	1980	219	912	4.2	8
10.	Darrin Nelson	1985	200	893	4.5	5

Rushing Days

Rank	Player	Att.	Yds.	TD	Opp./Date
1.	Chuck Foreman	28	200	2	at Philadelphia * 10-24-1976
2.	Ted Brown	29	179	1	at Green Bay * 10-23-1983
3.	Terry Allen	33	172	0	at Pittsburgh * 12-20-1992
4.	Robert Smith	16	169	1	at Buffalo * 8-31-1997
5.	Scottie Graham	33	166	1	Kansas City * 12-26-1993
6.	Robert Smith	17	160	0	Indianapolis * 12-21-1997
7.	Terry Allen	22	159	2	at Chicago Bears * 9-18-1994
8.	Chuck Foreman	33	156	2	at Detroit * 12-17-1977
9(t).	Dave Osborn	21	155	1	Green Bay * 12-3-1967
9(t).	Clinton Jones	22	155	1	Atlanta * 11-28-1971

100-Yard Rushing Games (Career)

Rank	Player	Seasons	Total
1.	Chuck Foreman	1973-79	17
2.	Robert Smith	1993-97	12
3.	Terry Allen	1990-94	7
4(t).	Tommy Mason	1961-66	6
4(t).	Dave Osborn	1965-75	6
4(t).	Ted Brown	1979-86	6
4(t).	Darrin Nelson	1982-89, 1991-92	6
8.	Herschel Walker	1989-91	4
9.	Scottie Graham	1991-95	3
10(t).	Clinton Jones	1967-72	2
10(t).	Alfred Anderson	1984-91	2
10(t).	Leroy Heard	1996-97	2

Receptions (Career)

Rank	Player	Seasons	Rec.	Yds.	Ave.	TD
1.	Cris Carter	1990-97	667	7,986	12.0	70
2.	Steve Jordan	1982-94	498	6,307	12.7	29
3.	Anthony Carter	1985-93	478	7,636	16.0	52
4.	Ahmad Rashad	1976-82	400	5,489	13.7	34
5.	Sammy White	1976-86	393	6,400	16.3	50
6.	Ted Brown	1979-86	339	2,850	8.4	13
7.	Chuck Foreman	1973-79	336	3,057	9.1	23
8.	Jake Reed	1992-97	308	5,007	16.3	26
9.	Rickey Young	1978-83	292	2,255	7.6	14
10.	Bill Brown	1962-74	284	3,177	11.2	23

Receptions (Season)

Rank	Player	Season	Att.	Yds.	Ave.	TD
1.	Cris Carter	1995	122	1,371	11.2	17
2.	Cris Carter	1994	122	1,256	10.3	7
3.	Cris Carter	1996	96	1,163	12.1	10
4.	Cris Carter	1997	89	1,069	12.0	13
5.	Rickey Young	1978	88	705	8.0	5
6.	Cris Carter	1993	86	1,071	12.5	9
7.	Jake Reed	1994	85	1,175	13.8	4
8.	Ted Brown	1981	83	836	8.4	2
9.	Ahmad Rashad	1979	80	1,156	14.5	9
10.	Chuck Foreman	1975	75	736	19.5	9

Receiving Yardage (Season)

Rank	Player	Season	Rec.	Yds.	Ave.	TD
1.	Cris Carter	1995	122	1,371	11.2	17
2.	Jake Reed	1996	72	1,320	18.3	7
3.	Cris Carter	1994	122	1,256	10.3	7
4.	Anthony Carter	1988	72	1,225	17.0	6
5.	Jake Reed	1994	85	1,175	13.8	4
6.	Jake Reed	1995	72	1,167	16.2	9
7.	Cris Carter	1996	96	1,163	12.1	10
8.	Ahmad Rashad	1979	80	1,156	14.5	9
9.	Jake Reed	1997	68	1,138	16.7	6
10.	Ahmad Rashad	1980	69	1,095	15.9	5

Receiving Days (Yardage)

Rank	Player	Rec.	Yds.	TD	Opp./Date
1.	Sammy White	7	210	1	Detroit * 11-7-1976
2.	Paul Flatley	6	202	2	at San Francisco * 10-24-1965
3.	Anthony Carter	8	188	2	Detroit * 11-6-1988
4.	Anthony Carter	8	184	1	at Dallas * 11-29-1987
5.	Steve Jordan	6	179	1	at Washington * 11-2-1986
6.	Sammy White	10	177	3	Chicago Bears * 11-28-1982
7.	Paul Flatley	6	174	1	Detroit * 11-24-1963
8.	Gene Washington	6	172	2	Baltimore Colts * 9-29-1969
9.	Cris Carter	14	167	0	at Arizona * 10-2-1994
10.	Anthony Carter	10	164	1	San Diego * 11-7-93

100-Yard Receiving Games (Career)

Rank	Player	Seasons	Total
1.	Cris Carter	1990-97	25
2.	Anthony Carter	1985-93	22
3.	Jake Reed	1991-97	15
4(t).	John Gilliam	1972-75	13
4(t).	Sammy White	1976-86	13
6.	Ahmad Rashad	1976-82	12
7(t).	Paul Flatley	1963-67	7
7(t).	Hassan Jones	1986-92	7
9.	Gene Washington	1967-72	6
10(t).	Joe Senser	1979-84	4
10(t).	Chuck Foreman	1973-79	4

Scoring (Career)

Rank	Player	Seasons	TD	FG	PAT	Pts.
1.	Fred Cox	1963-77	0	288	519	1,365
2.	Fuad Reveiz	1990-94	0	107	155	476
3.	Bill Brown	1962-74	76	0	0	456
4.	Chuck Foreman	1973-79	75	0	0	450
5.	Cris Carter	1990-97	70	0	10	430
6.	Rick Danmeier	1978-83	0	70	70	364
7.	Anthony Carter	1985-93	54	0	0	324
8.	Ted Brown	1979-86	53	0	0	318
9.	Sammy White	1976-86	50	0	0	300
10.	Chuck Nelson	1986-88	0	55	128	293

Scoring (Season)

Rank	Player	Season	TD	FG	PAT	Pts.
1(t).	Chuck Foreman	1975	22	0	0	132
1(t).	Fuad Reveiz	1994	0	34	30	132
3.	Fred Cox	1970	0	30	35	125
4.	Fuad Reveiz	1995	0	26	44	122
5.	Fred Cox	1969	0	26	43	121
6.	Rich Karlis	1989	0	31	27	120
7.	Fred Cox	1965	0	23	44	113
8.	Chuck Nelson	1986	0	22	44	110
9(t).	Chuck Nelson	1988	0	20	48	108
9(t).	Benny Ricardo	1983	0	25	33	108

Punting Average (Career -- Minimum 50 Att.)

Rank	Player	No.	Yds.	Ave.	Seasons
1.	Harry Newsome	308	13,501	43.8	1990-93
2.	Bobby Walden	258	11,067	42.9	1964-67
3.	Mike Saxon	149	6,249	41.9	1994-95
4.	Mitch Berger	161	6,749	41.9	1996-97
5.	Greg Coleman	721	29,391	40.8	1978-87
6.	Bucky Scribner	176	7,078	40.2	1987-89
7.	Mike Mercer	82	3,285	40.1	1961-62
8.	Neil Clabo	225	8,977	40.0	1975-77
9.	Bob Lee	156	6,205	39.8	1969-72, 1975-78
10.	Mike Eischeid	201	7,913	39.4	1972-74

Punting Average (Season)

Rank	Player	No.	Yds.	Ave.	Season
1.	Bobby Walden	72	3,341	46.4	1964
2.	Harry Newsome	68	3,094	45.5	1991
3.	Harry Newsome	72	3,240	45.0	1992
4.	Mike Mercer	19	826	43.5	1962
5.	Harry Newsome	90	3,861	42.9	1993
6.	Mike Saxon	77	3,301	42.9	1994
7.	Mitch Berger	73	3,133	42.9	1997
8.	Greg Coleman	67	2,869	42.8	1985
9.	Mike Eischeid	62	2,648	42.7	1972
10.	Greg Coleman	82	3,478	42.4	1984

Tackles (Career)

Rank	Player	Total	Solo	Assisted	Seasons
1.	Scott Studwell	1,981	1,308	673	1977-90
2.	Matt Blair	1,452	986	466	1974-85
3.	Jeff Siemon	1,382	1,008	374	1972-82
4.	Alan Page	1,120	868	252	1967-78
5.	Joey Browner	1,098	743	355	1977-84
6.	Tommy Hannon	1,096	728	368	1977-84
7.	Fred McNeill	1,068	682	386	1974-85
8.	Jim Marshall	988	719	269	1961-79
9.	Carl Eller	968	766	202	1964-78
10.	Roy Winston	894	689	205	1962-76

Tackles (Season)

Rank	Player	Total	Solo	Assisted	Season
1.	Scott Studwell	230	156	74	1981
2.	Jeff Siemon	229	170	59	1978
3.	Scott Studwell	133	83	216	1983
4.	Scott Studwell	215	143	72	1984
5.	Scott Studwell	207	153	54	1980
6.	Scott Studwell	206	109	97	1985
7.	Mike Merriweather	189	101	88	1991
8.	Jack Del Rio	185	118	67	1994
9.	Tommy Hannon	174	127	47	1979
10.	Scott Studwell	173	102	71	1989

Quarterback Sacks (Career)

Rank	Player	Seasons	Total
1.	Carl Eller	1964-78	130.0
2.	Jim Marshall	1961-79	127.0
3.	Alan Page	1967-78	108.0
4.	John Randle	1990-97	85.5
5.	Chris Doleman	1985-93	84.5
6.	Doug Martin	1980-89	60.5
7.	Henry Thomas	1987-94	56.0
8.	Keith Millard	1985-91	53.0
9.	Mark Mullaney	1975-87	41.5
10.	Gary Larsen	1965-74	37.0

Quarterback Sacks (Season)

Rank	Player	Seasons	Total
1.	Chris Doleman	1989	21.0
2(t).	Alan Page	1976	18.0
2(t).	Keith Millard	1989	18.0
4.	John Randle	1997	15.5
5(t).	Carl Eller	1969	15.0
5(t).	Carl Eller	1977	15.0
7.	Chris Doleman	1992	14.5
8.	John Randle	1994	13.5
9(t).	Jim Marshall	1969	13.0
9(t).	Carl Eller	1970	13.0
9(t).	Alan Page	1975	13.0

Interceptions (Career)

Rank	Player	Years	Int.	Yds.	Ave.	TD
1.	Paul Krause	1968-79	53	852	16.1	2
2.	Bobby Bryant	1967-80	51	749	14.7	3
3.	Ed Sharockman	1962-72	40	804	20.1	3
4.	Joey Browner	1983-91	37	465	12.6	3
5.	Nate Wright	1971-80	31	272	8.8	0
6.	John Turner	1978-85	22	227	10.3	1
7(t).	Audray McMillian	1989-93	19	227	11.9	3
7(t).	Karl Kassaulke	1963-72	19	187	9.8	0
9.	Orlando Thomas	1995-97	16	166	10.4	1

Interceptions (Season)

Rank	Player	Season	Int.	Yds.	Ave.	TD
1.	Paul Krause	1975	10	201	20.1	0
2(t).	Orlando Thomas	1995	9	108	12.0	1
2(t).	Audray McMilliam	1992	8	157	19.6	2
2(t).	Carl Lee	1988	8	118	14.8	2
2(t).	Bobby Bryant	1969	8	97	12.1	0
2(t).	Issiac Holt	1986	8	54	6.8	0
7(t).	Charlie West	1971	7	236	33.7	0
7(t).	Ed Sharockman	1970	7	132	18.8	1
7(t).	Bobby Bryant	1973	7	105	15.0	1
7(t).	Joey Browner	1990	7	103	14.7	1

Randall McDaniel

Robert Smith

Jake Reed

Todd Steussie

THE ANSWERS

Chapter 1 - IN THE BEGINNING

1. Minneapolis Marines (1921-24), Duluth Kelleys (1923-25), Duluth Eskimos (1926-27) and Minneapolis Red Jackets (1929-30).

2. In 1926, the Eskimos had only 15 players, including Ernie Nevers. That season, the team played 29 games—14 league games and 15 exhibitions—with 28 of those on the road. Nevers played all but 29 minutes of those games.

3. $15,000, the highest salary in the history of the NFL to that point.

4. Lamar Hunt of Dallas. He had unsuccessfully attempted to purchase the Chicago Cardinals in 1958, prompting his attempt to start a rival league.

5. Minnesota, Dallas, Houston, New York, Buffalo, Boston, Denver and Los Angeles.

6. Minneapolis.

7. Wisconsin quarterback Dale Hackbart. He later played for the Vikings (1966-70), but never played a down at quarterback in his 14-year NFL career.

8. The Oakland Raiders.

9. $60,000.

10. Joe Thomas, hired to be the team's head scout.

11. Nicollet Park in Minneapolis.

12. The Philadelphia Eagles played the Chicago Cardinals in a neutral site game to gauge Minnesota fan interest in the NFL Oct. 25, 1959. The Eagles won the game 28-24 in front of 20,112 fans.

13. Bloomington, Minnesota.

14. It was the first team in NFL history to be named after a state.

15. It was payment to the other NFL owners for the right to hold an expansion dispersal draft for players.

16. Bemidji, Minnesota, a town 250 miles north of Minneapolis.

17. Bud Grant and Ara Parseghian. Grant was coaching the Canadian Football League's Winnipeg Blue Bombers and Parseghian was coaching at Northwestern University.

18. Van Brocklin quarterbacked the Philadelphia Eagles to a 17-13 win over the Green Bay Packers. That game would prove to be the only championship game a Vince Lombardi coached team ever lost.

19. The Minneapolis Lakers.

20. The Minneapolis Minutemen.

Chapter 2 - THE DUTCHMAN AND HIS WAYWARD SONS

1. 30

2. Grady Alderman

3. "King of the Halfbacks"

4. $21,500

5. Minnesota, Baltimore, Chicago, Detroit, Green Bay, Los Angeles and San Francisco.

6. The game was played at Sioux Falls, South Dakota, Aug. 5, 1961. The Vikings lost 38-13 to the Dallas Cowboys.

7. Los Angeles Rams—the Rams won 27-17.

8. 41,200

9. It was the only stadium where both team benches were on the same side of the field.

10. Quarterback George Shaw and running backs Mel Triplett and Hugh McElhenny.

11. In 1961. The Vikings traded their first pick in the 1962 draft to acquire Shaw.

12. Bob Schnelker, later an offensive coordinator in Minnesota.

13. Kicker Mike Mercer with a first quarter field goal.

14. Fran Tarkenton and Rip Hawkins

15. Hugh McElhenny and Jerry Reichow

16. Olympic gymnast Cathy Rigby

17. $12,000

18. King was known as "The Chief"; Brown was called "Boom Boom".

19. St. Paul's Midway Stadium.

20. Hugh McElhenny

21. Ray Hayes on Dec. 3, 1961, vs. the Rams.

22. Ron Vanderkellen

23. Tommy Mason

24. Paul Flatley and Chuck Foreman

25. Billy Butler

26. Don Hultz

27. Jim Marshall is first with 29 and Carl Eller is third with 23. Chicago linebacker Dick Butkus is second on the all-time list.

28. "The Philosopher"

29. Running back

30. He was the co-inventor of the "Moon Ball," which was later trademarked under the name "Nerf Football."

31. He was general manager for the Calgary Stampeders of the Canadian Football League.

32. 47,200

33. Minnesota, Chicago, Detroit and Green Bay.

34. 29-51-4

35. Clinton Jones and Bob Grim in 1967, Ron Yary in 1968 and Ed White in 1969.

36. Yary's selection was the first overall pick in the 1968 draft.

37. March 10, 1967

Chapter 3 - THIS BUD'S FOR YOU

1. Superior, Wisconsin

2. University of Minnesota

3. Three each in baseball, basketball and football.

4. Harold Peter Grant Jr.

5. Winnipeg Blue Bombers

6. Four

7. Ron Vanderkellen

8. Milt Sunde

9. Football and basketball.

10. Basketball. He played with the Minneapolis Lakers under head coach Dave MacMillan.

11. Philadelphia Eagles

12. Wide receiver. He had 56 receptions for 997 yards and 7 touchdowns in only 12 games.

13. 158-96-5

14. Don Shula (67.6 percent), George Halas (67.1 percent), Earl "Curly" Lambeau (62.4 percent) and Paul Brown (62.1 percent).

15. Dallas running back Tony Dorsett, San Francisco defensive back Jimmy Johnson, Cleveland running back Leroy Kelly, former St. Louis and Dallas tight end Jackie Smith and Dallas defensive tackle Randy White.

CHAPTER 4 - THE GLORY YEARS

1. In a trade with the Los Angeles Rams after the Vikings' 1965 first-round draft pick—wide receiver Jack Snow—refused to sign.

2. New Orleans—No. 1 picks in 1968 and 1969.

3. Three games.

4. Tight end Billy Martin on a 1-yard touchdown pass from Joe Kapp.

5. NFL Playoff Bowl.

6. The Vikings lost 17-13 to Dallas at the Orange Bowl in Miami. Kapp later referred to that game, which was disbanded after the 1968 season, as "The Toilet Bowl."

7. Gary Cuozzo

8. Dave Osborn, Gene Washington twice, Bob Grim, Kent Kramer, John Beasley and Jim Lindsey.

9. Vice President Spiro Agnew

10. The game was played at the University of Minnesota's Memorial Stadium, because the Minnesota Twins were playing the Baltimore Orioles in the American League playoffs that day at Met Stadium. It was the first regular-season home game for the Vikings that wasn't played at Met Stadium and was the first NFL regular-season game ever played in a Big 10 stadium.

11. "Best wishes from ALL the Minnesota Vikings."

12. They lost to former coach Norm Van Brocklin.

13. He said there was no most valuable Viking, there were 40 most valuable Vikings.

14. Dave Osborn

15. Dave Osborn with 108 yards.

16. Gene Washington

17. Offensive coordinator Jerry Burns. He had coached under Vince Lombardi for the Packers in Super Bowls I and II.

18. It was his last game in a Viking uniform.

19. Kansas City in a rematch of the Super Bowl. The Vikings won 27-10.

20. Green Bay 13-10 at Milwaukee and the New York Jets 20-10 at Met Stadium.

21. Paul Krause on a 22-yard fumble return.

22. 31 games.

23. Fred Cox. He led the NFL in scoring for the second straight year by scoring 125 points—the most ever scored by a Viking in a 14-game schedule.

24. It allowed only two rushing touchdowns that season.

25. The team had records of 12-2 in 1969, 1970, 1973 and 1975 and 11-2-1 in 1976.

26. It allowed only 12 yards rushing in the game.

27. Six

28. Least points allowed.

29. The Boston Patriots were quarterbacked by Joe Kapp, and the Atlanta Falcons were coached by Norm Van Brocklin.

30. Bob Lee

31. Fred Cox kicked a 27-yard field goal, Alan Page sacked Roger Staubach for a safety and Stu Voigt caught a 6-yard touchdown pass from Gary Cuozzo.

32. Quarterback Norm Snead, wide receiver Bob Grim, running back Vince Clements, a No. 1 draft pick in 1972 and a No. 2 pick in 1973, who became defensive end Larry Jacobson and linebacker Brad Van Pelt.

33. $125,000

34. Charlie West, Gene Washington and Clinton Jones. Washington and Jones were gone after the 1972 season and West was gone after 1973—a testament to the lack of leverage players had in those days.

35. 1-5. The Vikings split with Green Bay and lost to San Francisco, Miami, Pittsburgh and Washington.

36. 14 games—5-0 in the pre-season and 9-0 to start the regular season.

37. Jesse "The Body" Ventura.

38. 161

39. 97 games. The next team to shut them out was the last team to do it—Cincinnati shut out the Vikings 14-0 Oct. 19, 1980.

40. Four times: 30 points at San Diego Dec. 5, 1971; 41 points at Los Angeles against the Rams Nov. 19, 1972 (a game the Vikes won 45-41); 27 points at Cincinnati Dec. 2, 1973; and 31 points at Washington Nov. 30, 1975.

41. Yale Stadium in New Haven, Connecticut.

42. John Gilliam on passes of 28 and eight yards.

43. It was the only time the Vikings won an NFC Championship Game on the road.

44. Four times. He was also named NFL MVP in 1971, the only time a defensive tackle ever won the honor.

45. 199

46. Paul Krause

47. He was trying to get an expansion franchise in Memphis, Tennessee.

48. They won both games—7-6 over Detroit and 11-7 over Chicago.

49. November, 1979—a span of 160 games.

50. John Gilliam on passes of 16 and 38 yards.

51. Jim Lash on a 29-yard pass from Fran Tarkenton and Dave Osborn on a 4-yard run.

52. Detroit beat Cleveland.

53. Nine—Bobby Bryant, Chuck Foreman, John Gilliam, Paul Krause, Alan Page, Jeff Siemon, Fran Tarkenton, Ed White and Ron Yary.

54. 377 points, an average of 27 points a game—still a team record average.

55. 10

56. Washington with a 31-30 win at RFK Stadium.

57. Armen Terzian

58. Ole Haugsrud, the owner of the Duluth Eskimos who had a prior claim to any NFL team that would return to Minnesota.

59. 73 points, while scoring 152 points.

60. 46-9-1

61. 52 games. The streak was broken when the team lost consecutive games to Seattle and the L.A. Rams in October, 1978.

62. 17-3-1

63. 17-5

64. Chuck Foreman and Brent McClanahan

65. Sammy White on catches of 27 and nine yards and Stu Voigt on an 18-yard reception.

66. Six games, 4-2 record.

Chapter 5 - CLOSE BUT NO CIGAR

1. Super Bowls IV, VIII, IX and XI.

2. New Orleans' Tulane Stadium.

3. Houston's Rice Stadium.

4. New Orleans' Tulane Stadium.

5. Pasadena's Rose Bowl.

6. It was the first Super Bowl attended by more than 100,000 fans (103,438).

7. Los Angeles Rams 23-20 and Cleveland 27-7.

8. New York Jets 13-6 and Oakland 17-7.

9. 13 or 14 points—depending on the source.

10. Kicker Jan Stenerud hit field goals of 48, 32 and 25 yards.

11. Charlie West fumbled it and Remi Prudhomme recovered.

12. Running back Mike Garrett on a 5-yard run.

13. Running back Dave Osborn on a 4-yard run.

14. Otis Taylor and Earsell Mackbee.

15. Willie Lanier, Johnny Robinson and Emmitt Thomas.

16. 39 yards on 11 carries.

17. Bill Brown, 26 yards on six carries.

18. Wide receiver John Henderson.

19. Hub Meads

20. Larry Csonka on a 5-yard run.

21. Jim Kiick on a 1-yard run.

22. Oscar Reed fumbled and Jake Scott recovered.

23. Larry Csonka on a 2-yard run.

24. Fran Tarkenton on a 4-yard run.

25. Most carries (33) and most rushing yards (145).

26. Oscar Reed, 11 carries 32 yards.

27. Seven attempts, six completions, 73 yards, no touchdowns, no interceptions.

28. Chuck Foreman

29. Dwight White scored a safety, tackling Fran Tarkenton in the end zone.

30. It was the first safety in Super Bowl history and remains the lowest halftime score in the history of the Super Bowl.

31. Bill Brown fumbled and Marv Kellom recovered.

32. Franco Harris on a 9-yard run.

33. Matt Blair blocked it, Terry Brown recovered it and former Viking punter Bobby Walden kicked it.

34. Linebacker Wally Hilgenberg.

35. Larry Brown on a 4-yard pass from Terry Bradshaw.

36. 119 total yards, 17 yards rushing.

37. Six—three by L.C. Greenwood.

38. Most carries (34) and most rushing yards (158)—breaking records set by Larry Csonka the previous year.

39. 22 yards on 12 carries.

40. Eleven

41. Wally Hilgenberg, Alan Page and Bob Lurtsema.

42. 81 million

43. A 24-yard field goal by Erroll Mann, a 1-yard pass to Dave Casper from Ken Stabler and a 1-yard run by Pete Banaszak.

44. Sammy White caught an 8-yard pass from Fran Tarkenton.

45. Banaszak on a 2-yard run.

46. Willie Davis scored on a 75-yard interception return—still the longest interception return for a touchdown in Super Bowl history.

47. Stu Voigt on a 13-yard pass from Bob Lee—who replaced Fran Tarkenton late in the game.

48. It was the first time Raider punter Ray Guy had a kick blocked in his pro career. Fred McNeill got the historic block.

49. He missed two extra points.

50. Clarence Davis

51. Len Dawson

52. Larry Csonka

53. Franco Harris

54. Fred Biletnikoff

55. None. Miami and Dallas had each played in three Super Bowls.

56. Don Shula (six) and Tom Landry (five).

57. Craig Morton

58. Tarkenton—both fumbles were his.

59. Miami in a 24-3 loss to Dallas in Super Bowl VI.

60. Nine first downs against Pittsburgh.

61. They did it three times—against Kansas City, Pittsburgh and Oakland. (For the record, they had five against Miami). The record was later broken by New England, which was limited to one by Chicago in Super Bowl XX.

62. Yes

Chapter 6 - THEY'RE BREAKING UP THAT OLD GANG OF MINE

1. They played the teams in the pre-season, regular season and post-season in the same year. For the record, the Vikings were 2-1 vs. the Rams, 3-0 vs. St. Louis, and 1-2 vs. Washington.

2. Sept. 22, 1967, in a 39-3 loss to the Rams at Los Angeles.

3. Fred McNeill

4. Nine

5. The first overtime win was a 22-16 victory vs. Chicago Oct. 17, 1977, at Met Stadium. The first OT loss was 16-10 loss at Dallas, Sept. 18, 1977.

6. 24-7

7. While Kramer was warming up to come into the game, Bob Lee led the team on its first scoring drive of the game—only to get pulled.

8. Sammy White

9. Bob Lee

10. Chuck Foreman and Sammy Johnson.

11. Chuck Foreman, with 101 yards.

12. Fred Cox on field goals of 33 and 37 yards.

13. Golden Richards on a 32-yard pass from Roger Staubach, Robert Newhouse on a 5-yard run and Tony Dorsett on an 11-yard run.

14. It was the Vikings' first loss in four NFC championship games.

15. Six. In those six games, the Vikings had outscored the Saints 175-41.

16. Tampa Bay won 16-10. It was not only the first division win for the Bucs in franchise history, it was their first win on the road.

17. Seattle, making the Vikings the first team to lose to both expansion franchises.

18. It was their seventh straight win—the longest winning streak against the Packers in team history. The Vikings did add two more games to that before losing the following year, but the winning streak stopped at seven with a 10-10 tie Nov. 26, 1978.

19. 1967

20. It had never been done before in NFL history.

21. It was tied 10-10.

22. Rick Danmeier kicked a 42-yard field goal and Ahmad Rashad caught a 1-yard pass from Fran Tarkenton.

23. 4-0

24. Two came on Pat Haden passes—a 9-yarder to wide receiver Willie Miller and a 27-yarder to wide receiver Ron Jessie—and two came on 3-yard scoring runs—one by Cullen Bryant and one by Jim Jodat.

25. Safety Bill Simpson

26. He called three running plays up the middle to kill the clock. He told reporters afterward he didn't want to jeopardize anyone's career on a meaningless play in the final minute of a game that had long since been decided.

27. 32

28. Attempts (572), completions (345) and yards (3,468).

29. 749

30. Running back Rickey Young with 88.

31. Kicker Rick Danmeier, punter Greg Coleman and return man Kevin Miller.

32. Four times—1969, 1973, 1977 and 1978.

33. Three times—1968, 1972 and 1975.

34. Defensive end Mark Mullaney.

35. Page led six times, Eller five times and Marshall six times. Marshall tied for the team lead at 10.5 with Don Hultz in 1963.

36. Oct. 6, 1963 in a 56-14 loss to the St. Louis Cardinals.

37. 17

38. Four

39. 20-1

40. Nine

41. 6-3

42. 5-3

43. Green Bay in 1972 and Tampa Bay in 1979.

44. Safety Tommy Hannon.

45. Larry Vargo

46. 23

47. Rickey Young

48. In October, 1965, scoring 38 vs. the Rams, 40 vs. the Giants and 37 vs. the Bears. That team actually did it four times, tacking on 42 points vs. the 49ers the following week.

49. Ahmad Rashad, Sammy White and Terry LeCount.

50. Cleveland defensive back Thom Darden.

51. "5,000 bucks!", a reference to how much money the Vikings' players each earned for making the playoffs.

52. Most completions (38, a record that still stands), and 456 yards passing.

53. The Vikings led 14-0.

54. Sammy White on a 30-yard pass from Tommy Kramer, Ted Brown on a 1-yard run and a safety shared on a sack of Ron Jaworski by Matt Blair and Doug Martin.

55. Three

56. Three

57. Eight—the three fumbles and five interceptions by Kramer.

58. Eddie Payton

59. Scott Studwell

60. 1967, when the team started 0-4.

61. 1975, when the team started 10-0.

62. 1962, when the team started 0-5. The only longer streak was in the inaugural season, 1961, when the team lost seven straight.

63. In 1962—the only time it had happened. The Vikings scored seven points in each of their first three games that year and were shut out in the fourth.

64. Ted Brown

65. Ted Brown

66. Winter Park in Eden Prairie, Minnesota.

67. Ted Brown, on a 6-yard run against Green Bay Nov. 29, 1981.

68. Rick Danmeier on a 33-yard field goal against Kansas City Dec. 20, 1981.

69. The Mall of America, the largest shopping

mall in the United States.

Chapter 7 - THERE"S NO PLACE LIKE DOME

1. Minnesota senator and former Vice President Hubert H. Humphrey.

2. Aug. 21, 1982

3. Seattle. The Vikings won 7-3.

4. Tight end Joe Senser caught an 11-yard pass from Tommy Kramer.

5. Tampa Bay. The Vikings won 17-10.

6. Rickey Young on a 3-yard run.

7. They played four games and went 3-1—beating Chicago, Tampa Bay and Detroit and losing to Green Bay.

8. 4-1, losing only to the New York Jets.

9. No. 4

10. 30-24 Vikings.

11. Their offense didn't score. Atlanta got its points on a blocked punt, an interception return and a 17-yard run by kicker Mick Luckhurst on a fake field goal.

12. Five times.

13. Sammy White and Sam McCullum.

14. Ted Brown on a 5-yard run.

15. 21-7

16. John Riggins. He had 37 carries for 185 yards and a touchdown.

17. Ted Brown on an 18-yard run.

18. Jarvis Redwine

19. It was almost 20 years since the Vikings gave up 56 points against St. Louis Oct. 6, 1963.

20. Both were overtime wins. It was the first time the Vikings won two overtime games in one year.

21. The final was 13-2—the Vikings only points coming on a safety.

22. Benny Ricardo

23. Running back Darrin Nelson.

24. Steve Dils

25. Atlanta, Detroit and Tampa Bay.

26. Buffalo and Houston.

27. Eight, including the last six.

28. 10, including the last four.

29. Alfred Anderson

30. Leo Lewis

31. Randy Holloway and Charlie Johnson

32. San Francisco. The 49ers were the defending Super Bowl champions.

33. It was the first time Green Bay swept the

Vikings two years in a row since winning the first six meetings between the teams from 1961-63.

34. The Vikings trailed 23-0 with 8:30 to play in the game.

35. Jan Stenerud

36. Buster Rhymes

37. Green Bay's Vince Lombardi

38. Offensive coordinator Bob Schnelker and defensive coordinator Floyd Peters.

39. He threw for a team-record 490 yards, becoming the first player in NFL history to top 450 yards twice in his career.

40. They played Green Bay in front of 13,911 fans.

41. Tony Adams

42. Then-Viking assistant coach Marc Trestman.

43. $1 million a year.

44. The Vikings beat Denver 34-27. The game was played on Monday because the stadium was in use Sunday as the Minnesota Twins defeated the St. Louis Cardinals in Game 7 of the 1987 World Series. The same situation would happen 10 years later when Miami and Chicago played a second Monday Night Football game because the Florida Marlins were playing a World Series game.

45. 8-4

46. 12-3

47. Anthony Carter brought a punt back 84 yards for a touchdown to set a post-season record.

48. Tight end Steve Jordan on a 5-yard pass from Wade Wilson, Anthony Carter on a 10-yard pass from running back Allen Rice and Hassan Jones on a 44-yard pass from Wade Wilson.

49. Chuck Nelson

50. D.J. Dozier

51. 41 minutes, 18 seconds

52. Six—four interceptions and two fumbles

53. An NFL-best 13-2

54. Tight end Carl Hilton on a 7-yard pass from Wade Wilson, Chuck Nelson's 23-yard field goal and defensive back Reggie Rutland's 45-yard interception return.

55. Chuck Nelson on field goals of 40, 46 and 23 yards and wide receiver Hassan Jones on a 5-yard pass from Wade Wilson.

56. He piled up 227 receiving yards on 10 receptions.

57. Running back Kelvin Bryant on a 42-yard pass

from Doug Williams.

58. Leo Lewis on a 23-yard pass from Wade Wilson.

59. Gary Clark on a 7-yard pass from Doug Williams.

60. Cornerback Darrell Green

61. Eight times

62. Wheelock Whitney, Jaye Dyer, Carl Pohlad and Irwin Jacobs.

63. Seven

64. One—Chicago was 12-4, forcing the Vikings to be a wild card despite and 11-5 record.

65. Joey Browner

66. Alfred Anderson on a 7-yard run and Allen Rice on a 17-yard run.

67. Alfred Anderson on a 1-yard run and Carl Hilton on a 5-yard pass from Wade Wilson.

68. Jerry Rice on passes of 2, 4 and 11 yards from Joe Montana.

69. Hassan Jones on a 5-yard pass from Wade Wilson.

70. Running back Roger Craig on runs of 4 and 80 yards.

71. Carl Lee

72. Darryl Harris

73. Bucky Scribner

74. Anthony Carter, with 1,225 yards on 72 receptions.

75. Darrin Nelson

76. Linebackers Jesse Solomon and David Howard, cornerback Issiac Holt, defensive end Alex Stewart and running back Darrin Nelson—who refused to report to Dallas and was traded to San Diego.

77. None of them actually ended up with Dallas, since the Cowboys used the picks to make trades the produced Russell Maryland and Emmitt Smith. The picks given up by the Vikings were: 1990—tight end Eric Green of Pittsburgh; 1991—offensive tackle Pat Harlow of New England; 1992—offensive tackle Eugene Chung of New England.

78. Tight end Mike Jones in 1990 and wide receiver Jake Reed in 1991.

79. They were one-point losses—10-9 at Philadelphia and 20-19 at Green Bay.

80. The Vikings won 23-21 in overtime—the only NFL overtime game ever decided by a safety.

81. Nine

82. Chicago won five times and Detroit and Tampa Bay won one each. Technically, the Packers won in 1982, but, because of the nine-game season, teams were simply divided by conference, not divisions, to select playoff teams.

83. Jerry Rice on receptions of 72 and 13 yards and 8-yard passes to Brent Jones and John Taylor.

84. Running back Rick Fenney.

85. Irwin Jacobs and Carl Pohlad.

86. $25 million.

87. Lynn set up a one-man, one-vote system of voting. Despite Jacobs and Pohlad owning more than 50 percent of team stock, Lynn still controlled two-thirds of the voting stock.

88. $50 million.

89. Fran Tarkenton

90. After starting 1-1, they lost five straight, won five straight and lost the last four.

91. Cris Carter

92. He was cut by Philadelphia. The Vikings paid $100 to claim Carter.

93. Tampa Bay and Phoenix. The Vikings played Phoenix twice by virtue of a fifth-place schedule.

94. He was put in charge of the World League of American Football.

95. Roger Headrick

96. Exxon and Pillsbury.

97. Hiring Dennis Green as head coach.

98. Pete Carroll

Chapter 8 - GREEN ACRES

1. John Skoglund, Jaye Dyer, Phillip Maas, James Binger, N. Bud Grossman, Roger Headrick, James Jundt, Elizabeth MacMillan, Carol Sperry and Wheelock Whitney.

2. Dayton

3. Northwestern

4. 34

5. Receivers coach, where he tutored Jerry Rice.

6. Stanford

7. Notre Dame

8. Robert Smith

9. 10

10. Three, but two of them—Cris Carter and Randall McDaniel—were All-Pros.

11. 14

12. Nine

13. Todd Scott

14. Detroit 31-17 Sept. 13, 1992, at Detroit.

15. The beat Pittsburgh 6-3 Dec. 20 to clinch the Central Division and lost 15-13 to Washington Oct. 25.

16. Terry Allen on a 1-yard run.

17. Brian Mitchell. He gained 109 rushing yards.

18. Ernest Byner on a 3-yard run, Brian Mitchell on an 8-yard run and Gary Clark on a 24-yard pass from Mark Rypien.

19. 17 minutes, 17 seconds.

20. 57 yards—he had 56 yards on the game's opening drive.

21. Tampa Bay and Detroit.

22. It was the first Viking shutout in the Metrodome. The last home shutout was vs. Detroit in 1980 at Met Stadium.

23. 1971, when the Vikings had three shutouts.

24. Two

25. 8-3

26. The Vikings led 10-3.

27. Rodney Hampton on runs of 51 and two yards.

28. Linebacker Jack Del Rio

29. Plan B free agency from Dallas.

30. Eric Guliford

31. Harry Newsome

32. Nine

33. Scottie Graham

34. A No. 4 pick in 1994 and a No. 3 pick in 1995.

35. Cornerback Mike Davis in 1994 and running back Rodney Thomas in 1995.

36. Cody Carlson

37. Green Bay 16-10 at Green Bay and Arizona 17-7 at Arizona.

38. Lost 26-20 at New England and 20-17 vs. Tampa Bay and defeated Chicago 33-27 on Monday Night Football at the Metrodome.

39. 6-2

40. Sean Salisbury

41. Steve Walsh, who threw a 9-yard TD to tight end Keith Jennings and a 21-yard touchdown to wide receiver Jeff Graham.

42. Lewis Tillman on a 1-yard run and Raymont Harris on a 29-yard run.

43. Cris Carter on a 4-yard pass and Amp Lee on an 11-yarder.

44. 292 yards.

45. Amp Lee, who had 11 receptions for 159 yards.

46. Four turnovers and 11 penalties.

47. John Randle. He had tied Chris Doleman the previous year for the team lead with 12.5 sacks.

48. Anthony Parker and Vencie Glenn.

49. 132

50. Tommy Kramer, who threw for 3,912 yards in 1981.

51. Six—three by Chuck Foreman, two by Terry Allen and one by Ted Brown.

52. Green Bay 5-1, Chicago 6-0, Detroit 3-3 and Tampa Bay 4-2.

53. Pittsburgh (44) and New Orleans (43).

54. 11

55. 2-6

56. Jim Finks

57. Orlando Thomas. The other two were Rip Hawkins in 1961 and George Rose in 1964.

58. He was the first Viking to lead the NFL in interceptions, although Audray MacMillan tied for the NFL lead in 1992.

59. David Palmer joined Leo Lewis (1987), Charlie West (1968) and Billy Butler (1963).

60. Eddie Payton in 1981 and Lance Rentzel in 1965.

61. 33, breaking the record of 26 set by Tommy Kramer in 1981.

62. Max Winter

63. 1975

64. 4-0

65. 1-3

66. The Jacksonville Jaguars and the Baltimore Ravens. Although the Vikings had played Cleveland several times, the Ravens left the career statistics of the Browns in Cleveland for their next team.

67. London Monarchs of the World League of American Football.

68. Dallas led 30-0.

69. Safety George Teague

70. Cris Carter on a 30-yard pass from Brad Johnson and Johnson on a 5-yard run.

71. Cris Carter on a pass from Brad Johnson.

72. 1975, when they won 10 straight games.

73. "No Room For Crybabies"

74. Gene McGivern

75. 1984, when they lost their last six games to finish 3-13.

76. They scored 10 points in the final 90 seconds.

77. The Giants led 19-3.

78. They scored five times, but four of those were field goals.

79. Leroy Hoard on a 4-yard run.

80. Jake Reed on a 30-yard pass from Randall Cunningham.

81. It hit Chris Calloway and was recovered by Chris Walsh.

82. None

83. Running back Terry Kirby on a 1-yard run and linebacker Ken Norton Jr. on a 23-yard interception return.

84. Cris Carter on passes of 66 and three yards and wide receiver Matthew Hatchette on a 13-yard pass—all from Randall Cunningham.

85. Terry Kirby

86. Jake Reed

87. He topped 300 yards for the first time in playoff history, throwing for 331 yards.

88. $200 million.

89. $250 million

Chapter 9 - BY THE NUMBERS

1. Fran Tarkenton's No. 10 and Alan Page's No. 88.

2. Jim Marshall's No. 70 was worn for 19 seasons, while kicker Teddy Garcia was the only player to wear No. 2 (in 1989).

3. He started his career wearing No. 20, but changed it to No. 26 in 1994.

4. Linebacker Chris Martin (1984-88) wore Nos. 56, 57, 94 and 95.

5. No. 89 has been worn by 20 different players, most recently by wide receiver Matthew Hatchette.

6. Running backs Jim Young and Rickey Young both wore No. 34 and tight ends Steve Jordan and Andrew Jordan both wore No. 83 (Andrew gave up the number when Steve came out of retirement in the middle of the 1994 season).

7. Tommy Kramer's No. 9.

8. Warren Moon, Chuck Nelson, Benny Ricardo, and Gary Anderson.

9. Jan Stenerud (1984-85), Rich Karlis (1989) and Eddie Murray (1997).

10. Tony Adams and Randall Cunningham.

11. Punter Greg Coleman.

12. Quarterback King Hill in 1968, who was expected to be Tarkenton's replacement when he was traded to the New York Giants.

13. Joe Kapp and Wade Wilson.

14. George Shaw, Brad Johnson and Fred Cox.

15. Norm Snead and Rich Gannon.

16. Tommy Mason, Darrin Nelson and Robert Smith.

17. Hall of Famer Paul Krause.

18. Wide receiver Ahmad Rashad.

19. Running back Bill Brown.

20. Running back Roger Craig.

21. Todd Scott and Bob Tucker.

22. John Gilliam and D.J. Dozier.

23. Mick Tingelhoff

24. Scott Studwell and Jack Del Rio.

25. Milt Sunde and Randall McDaniel.

26. Grady Alderman

27. Ron Yary and Todd Steussie.

28. Bob Schnelker and Cris Carter.

29. Carl Eller and Anthony Carter.

30. Sammy White

31. Jerry Reichow

32. Jimmy Walker, a 1987 strike replacement player.

33. Henry Thomas

Matching

1-C

2-D

3-H

4-J

5-Q

6-G

7-K

8-E

9-N

10-F

11-B

12-M

13-A

14-O

15-I

16-P

17-L.

Chapter 10 - MINNESOTA'S ON THE CLOCK

1. Ed Sharockman

2. Roy Winston

3. Bobby Bell

4. Fred Cox

5. Carl Eller

6. The Chicago Bears

7. Jack Snow and Lance Rentzel.

8. Dave Osborn

9. Miami's Howard Twilley.

10. Clinton Jones, Gene Washington and Alan Page.

11. Bobby Bryant

12. Offensive tackle Ron Yary

13. Guard Ed White

14. Stu Voigt

15. Leo Hayden

16. Jeff Siemon

17. The draft pick was defensive back Jackie Wallace and the player acquired was wide receiver John Gilliam.

18. Chuck Foreman on the first round and Brent McClanahan on the fifth round.

19. Fred McNeill on the first round and Matt Blair on the second round.

20. Defensive end Mark Mullaney in 1975 and defensive tackle James "Duck" White in 1976.

21. Sammy White

22. Quarterback Tommy Kramer on the first round and linebacker Scott Studwell on the ninth round.

23. Defensive end Randy Holloway

24. Ted Brown

25. Defensive tackle Doug Martin

26. Wide receiver Mardye McDole, linebacker Robin Sendlein and running back Jarvis Redwine.

27. Offensive tackle Tim Irwin

28. Wade Wilson

29. San Francisco linebacker Jim Fahnhorst.

30. Gerald Riggs, Marcus Allen and Joe Morris.

31. Joey Browner

32. Carl Lee

33. Keith Millard in 1984 and Chris Doleman in 1985.

34. Kirk Lowdermilk and Steve Bono.

35. Gerald Robinson

36. Offensive tackle Gary Zimmerman

37. Anthony Carter

38. D.J. Dozier

39. Henry Thomas

40. Randall McDaniel and Todd Kalis

41. Quarterback Rich Gannon

42. They didn't draft a quarterback, a running back or a wide receiver.

43. They traded it to Pittsburgh for linebacker Mike Merriweather.

44. Terry Allen and John Randle.

45. Todd Scott in 1991 and Orlando Thomas in 1995.

46. Keith Millard

47. Linebacker Ed McDaniel on the fifth round and quarterback Brad Johnson on the ninth round.

48. Running back Robert Smith

49. Cornerback Dewayne Washington and offensive tackle Todd Steussie.

50. Defensive end Derrick Alexander and offensive tackle Korey Stringer.

51. Duane Clemons and Dwayne Rudd.

Chapter 11 - FOR THE RECORD

1. 18 players—13 to Dallas and five to the Vikings.

2. Three—San Francisco (16), Dallas (14) and Pittsburgh (14).

3. Only Dallas with 20. The Vikings are tied with Pittsburgh and San Francisco with 18 each.

4. Paul Hornung, Ken Houston, Willie Lanier and Doak Walker.

5. Fred Biletnikoff, Mike Ditka and Jack Ham.

6. Mike Singletary, Dwight Stephenson, Anthony Munoz and Tommy McDonald.

7. 4-2

8. Fran Tarkenton

9. Ahmad Rashad

10. It was the last game played somewhere other than Aloha Stadium in Hawaii. It was played at the Los Angeles Coliseum.

11. London

12. Goteborg, Sweden

13. They beat Buffalo 20-6 Aug. 7, 1993, in Tokyo and beat Kansas City 17-9 Aug. 6, 1994, in Berlin.

14. 16-17

15. 1981

16. 1980 and 1984-86.

17. San Francisco, which has played at least once every year since 1983, and Oakland, which has played at least once in every season of Monday Night Football.

18. A 99-yard run by Tony Dorsett of Dallas January 3, 1983.

19. Jerry Rice

20. Walker Lee Ashley

21. Eddie Payton on a 99-yard return vs. Oakland.

22. 27 games—the most of any team in the NFL.

23. 13-12-2

24. 1994 and 1995. The team went 2-2 both years.

25. Green Bay

26. Minnesota beat Chicago 22-16 Oct. 10, 1977, with a pass; lost 23-17 to Cleveland Dec. 17, 1989, on a pass; and lost 27-21 to the Los Angeles Rams Dec. 2, 1979, on a pass.

27. Warren Moon to Cris Carter on a 65-yard pass to beat Chicago 33-27 Dec. 1, 1994; Tommy Kramer to Ahmad Rashad on a 50-yarder to beat Green Bay 27-21 Sept. 23, 1979; and Moon to Qadry Ismail on a 50-yarder to beat Arizona 30-24 Nov. 12, 1995.

28. Kicker Jan Stenerud

29. Ron Yary and Carl Eller

30. George Blanda (26 years) and Earl Morrall (21 years).

31. Jim Marshall (282 games) and Mick Tingelhoff (240).

32. Fred Cox

33. Eddie Murray made 250 in a row to break the record held by San Francisco's Tommy Davis (234).

34. Rich Karlis made seven field goals Nov. 15, 1989, against the L.A. Rams, tying a record held by Jim Bakken of St. Louis and later Chris Boniol of Dallas.

35. Fred Cox—31 games.

36. Fuad Reveiz—31 straight.

37. Alan Page and Tommy Hannon.

38. New England's Drew Bledsoe threw 70 passes and completed 45 of them.

39. Sid Luckman (1943), Adrian Burk (1954), George Blanda (1961) and Y.A. Tittle (1962).

40. Rich Gannon—63 passes vs. New England Oct. 20, 1991.

41. Detroit's Herman Moore.

42. Jerry Rice with 22 in 1987 (in which he played only 12 games!), Mark Clayton with 18 in1984 and Sterling Sharpe with 18 in 1994.

43. Paul Krause

44. Leo Lewis

45. Jim Marshall recovered 29 fumbles.

46. Don Hultz recovered nine in 1963 and Alan Page recovered seven in 1970.

47. Buster Rhymes

48. The Los Angeles Rams from 1973-79.

49. Most pass attempts in a season with 709.

50. 10 times.

51. The team lost only three fumbles.

52. 31

53. 1969-71

54. Two

55. 71 sacks, one short of the record held by the 1984 Chicago Bears.

56. 53 touchdowns—17 in 1974, 22 in 1975 and 14 in 1976.

57. Fran Tarkenton (91.8 in 1975), Tommy Kramer (92.6 in 1986) and Wade Wilson (91.5 in 1988).

58. No Viking has ever led the NFL or NFC in rushing yardage.

59. No. Rickey Young caught 88 in 1978 and Chuck Foreman caught 73 in 1975 to lead the NFL.

60. No Viking has ever led the NFL in receiving yards.

61. 1969, when the team scored 379 points.

62. Dennis Green. He won his 96th game in the regular season finale of 1997 to pass Jerry Burns and move into second place.

63. Bill Brown and Ted Brown.

64. Chuck Foreman in 1974.

65. Jan Stenerud vs. Atlanta Sept. 16, 1984.

66. 200

67. Walter Payton (275), Barry Sanders (220), James Wilder (219) and Earl Campbell (203).

68. Robert Smith in 1997.

69. Warren Moon

70. Fran Tarkenton to wide receiver Charley Ferguson Nov. 11, 1962.

71. Rickey Young vs. New England Dec. 16, 1979.

72. Anthony Carter with 105 games.

73. Four straight years of teammates with 1,000-yard receiving seasons (they set the record when they did it twice).

74. Robert Smith with 415—a record that was intact at the end of the 1997 season.

75. Ed Sharockman, Bobby Bryant and Joey Browner.

76. Carl Eller with 130.

77. Chris Doleman with 21, one short of the record held by former New York Jet Mark Gastineau.

78. Matt Blair with 20.

79. Tommy Kramer with 19. The Vikings were 9-10 in those games.

80. Terry Allen. The Vikings went 7-0 when he rushed for 100 yards.
81. Wade Wilson (5-2) and Fran Tarkenton (6-3).
82. Chuck Foreman (4-0) and Ted Brown (3-0)
83. John Gilliam

Chapter 12 - BIG MAN ON CAMPUS

1. Detroit
2. Florida State
3. Clemson
4. Iowa State
5. Illinois
6. North Carolina State
7. USC
8. South Carolina
9. Michigan
10. Ohio State
11. Florida A & M
12. Nebraska
13. Sioux Falls
14. USC
15. Baylor
16. Pittsburgh
17. Minnesota
18. Northwestern
19. Miami (Florida)
20. South Carolina State
21. Indiana State
22. North Carolina
23. Iowa
24. Notre Dame
25. Clemson
26. Tennessee
27. Florida State
28. Brown
29. California
30. Drake
31. Concordia (Minn.)
32. Marshall
33. Ohio State
34. Ohio State
35. Washington
36. Tulane
37. Arizona State
38. Washington
39. Brigham Young
40. UCLA
41. Washington State
42. Washington
43. Colorado State
44. Stanford
45. North Dakota
46. Notre Dame
47. Texas A & I
48. Oregon
49. Grambling
50. Southwest Louisiana
51. West Chester
52. Pittsburgh
53. Stanford
54. California
55. Ohio State
56. Illinois
57. Minnesota
58. Superior (Wis.) State
59. Georgia
60. Louisiana State
61. Nebraska
62. Wisconsin
63. Tennessee Tech
64. Michigan State
65. Texas-El Paso
66. California
67. Grambling
68. East Texas State
69. Louisiana State
70. San Diego State
71. USC
72. Oregon

Chapter 13 - AND THE WINNER IS ...

1. Running back Tommy Mason
2. Center Mick Tingelhoff
3. Carl Eller
4. Offensive tackle Ron Yary
5. Six
6. Chuck Foreman, Paul Krause, Alan Page, Fran Tarkenton, Ed White and Ron Yary.
7. None
8. Matt Blair in 1980 and Doug Martin in 1982.
9. Joey Browner
10. Randall McDaniel
11. Randall McDaniel with seven and John Randle with five.
12. 1973 and 1975.
13. Six, five and zero.

14. Harry Newsome in 1992.

15. Fuad Reveiz in 1994.

16. Chris Doleman, Randall McDaniel, Audray MacMillian, Todd Scott, Gary Zimmerman and Harry Newsome.

17. Alan Page in 1971 and Fran Tarkenton in 1975.

18. Jim Finks in 1973.

19. Alan Page in 1971 and 1973 and Keith Millard in 1989.

20. Tommy Kramer in 1986.

21. Paul Flatley in 1963, Chuck Foreman in 1973 and Sammy White in 1976.

22. Mick Tingelhoff in 1969 and Ron Yary in 1975.

23. Running back Hugh McElhenny and wide receiver Jerry Reichow.

24. Tommy Mason, Grady Alderman and Rip Hawkins.

25. Tommy Mason (1962-64).

26. Mick Tingelhoff

27. Nine

28. All four were selected—Alan Page, Carl Eller and Jim Marshall were starters and Gary Larsen was selected as a reserve.

29. Alan Page with seven, and John Randle and Chris Doleman with five each.

30. It was a tie—Gary Larsen and Jim Marshall were each selected twice.

31. Carl Eller, Paul Krause, Jim Marshall, Alan Page, Mick Tingelhoff and Gene Washington.

32. Chuck Foreman, John Gilliam, Alan Page, Jeff Siemon, Ed White and Ron Yary. Fran Tarkenton was selected, but did not play.

33. Carl Eller in 1973.

34. Seven (1971-77).

35. He was hosting NBC-TV's new late night show "Saturday Night Live."

36. Matt Blair and Ahmad Rashad.

37. 1983

38. Joe Senser in 1981. An injury prevented him from playing.

39. Matt Blair in 1982, Jan Stenerud in 1984 and Joey Browner in 1985. Browner was selected as a special teams player.

40. The starters were Joey Browner, Anthony Carter, Chris Doleman, Carl Lee, Keith Millard and Gary Zimmerman. The reserves were Steve Jordan,

Scott Studwell and Wade Wilson.

41. 1986

42. Nine

43. Five

44. Quarterback Warren Moon in 1994 and 1995, linebacker Jack Del Rio in 1994 and kicker Fuad Reveiz in 1994.

45. Seven times. The others were tackle Grady Alderman, guard Milt Sunde and center Mick Tingelhoff in 1966, guard Ron Yary and tackle Ed White in 1975, 1976 and 1977, and McDaniel and tackle Gary Zimmerman in 1989 and 1992. In all, multiple Viking offensive lineman have been selected to a Pro Bowl as starters or reserves in 12 different seasons.

Chapter 14 - THE END OF THE ROAD

1. Cleveland Browns

2. Tampa Bay Buccaneers

3. Detroit Lions

4. Los Angeles Raiders

5. Washington Redskins

6. St. Louis Cardinals

7. Atlanta Falcons

8. Detroit Lions

9. Seattle Seahawks

10. Atlanta Falcons

11. New England Patriots

12. New Orleans Saints

13. New York Giants

14. New England Patriots

15. Dallas Cowboys

16. Miami Dolphins

17. San Diego Chargers

18. Kansas City Chiefs

19. Boston Patriots

20. New Orleans Saints

21. Los Angeles Rams

22. New Orleans Saints

23. Seattle Seahawks

24. Washington Redskins

25. Detroit Lions

26. Philadelphia Eagles

27. Indianapolis Colts

28. Green Bay Packers

29. Chicago Bears

30. Atlanta Falcons

31. San Diego Chargers

32. Tampa Bay Buccaneers

33. Seattle Seahawks

34. Atlanta Falcons

35. Denver Broncos

36. Denver Broncos

37. San Diego Chargers

38. Los Angeles Rams

Chapter 15 - THIS, THAT, AND THE OTHER

1. Jim Marshall

2. "Moose"

3. Red McCloud

4. Athens, Georgia

5. Fred Zamberletti

6. Jim "Stubby" Eason

7. "Chicano Joe"

8. Lexington, Nebraska

9. "Mooney"

10. George

11. He had a raging hangover from partying all night before the game.

12. He accidentally shot himself, almost froze to death when a snowmobiling party he was with got marooned in the mountains of Montana (one member of his party did die) and he crashed a motorized glider in a telephone pole and fell 40 feet to the ground.

13. They were playing the San Francisco 49ers at Kezar Stadium. Marshall ran 66 yards and was congratulated by 49er offensive lineman Bruce Bosley.

14. Tommy Mason, Clinton Jones, Chuck Foreman and D.J. Dozier

15. Bobby Moore

16. He called him "Hunkie", which means "stupid."

17. Paul Krause

18. The Oakland Invaders, the team that took over the Michigan Panthers when that franchise folded.

19. The Memphis Showboats. He began his USFL career with the Los Angeles Express, protecting a quarterback named Steve Young.

20. John Michels

21. The Sunset Music Band. The band released the CD "Sunset Celebration"—a project that included the author/producer of the classic bad song "Funky Town."

22. Karl Kassaulke and Earsell Mackbee.

23. "Crazy George"

24. Ragnar and Vikadontis Rex

25. "Chainsaw"

26. Grady Alderman

27. Camp Skywalker

28. "The Trashman"

29. The Viking team bus got caught in traffic outside the Lions stadium in Pontiac, Michigan.

30. 50 wins, 48 losses.

31. $10 million

32. A Columbus, Ohio, pharmacy.

33. He was given a tryout because his father, according to Grant, "was the best athlete I've ever seen" when Grant was coaching in the Canadian Football League. He gave Lewis a tryout as a favor to his father.

34. Tom Clancy.

ABOUT THE AUTHOR

John Holler is a native-born Minnesotan who has been following the Vikings since he first saw his father throw various objects at the TV screen during Super Bowl IV—introducing the youngster to words he had never heard before.

John has been a professional sports writer since 1990. Aside from his daily newspaper work as a sportswriter, John's work has appeared in *USA Today*, a pair of books—*War Stories From the Field* and *Hit and Tell: War Stories From the NFL's Wildest Players*—and Harris Publications, which produces a football magazine (*Blitz*), a basketball magazine (*Slam*), and a baseball magazine (*Hardball*). He has been a beat writer and columnist for *Bob Lurtsema's Viking Update* since 1989. John has also hosted a cable TV sports show, is a movie reviewer for WJON-AM radio in St. Cloud, Minn., and works as a government reporter for a Minnesota newspaper syndicate. Since 1989, John has written copy for *Top Dog Sports*—a fantasy football publication—which he recently optioned to a fantasy football website on the Internet.

John is married and he and his wife Dawn have one child—a daughter named Megan—who it is rumored is beginning to hear words she has never heard before when sitting in front of the TV with her father watching Vikings games.

The Ravenstone Story

G eoffrey Chaucer had a teacher named William Ravenstone, a man history would have forgotten had he not left an estate of 83 handwritten books when he died in late 1300s. This was great wealth—for the 14th Century. Translated into 20th Century terms, Ravenstone's collection was the equivalent of an average American high school library.

Ravenstone left his library to the school where he taught Chaucer and many other sons of England's nobility and gentry. To preserve his treasure, he also bequeathed a cedar chest to the school. The books were to be used by the students of the school. They could be borrowed from the library one at a time with the stipulations that they were to be read thoroughly and returned in the same condition in which they had been loaned.

Ravenstone understood the value of books. They were his fortune, the sum total of his life. He saw them as the path for communicating knowledge and ideas from one generation to the next, from one people to another. They were the creations of the wordsmith, that novelist or poet who revealed in the written word the depths of the human soul and the condition of humanity.

In pounds and pence, Ravenstone passed from this earth much as he had entered it. But he considered himself a man of means because he possessed books, more books than nearly every other man in all of England. He owned knowledge, ideas, and literature. Through them, he found immortality.

AUTOGRAPHS

John Holler

AUTOGRAPHS